PostGIS Essentials

Learn how to build powerful spatial database
solutions with PostGIS quickly and efficiently

Angel Marquez

BIRMINGHAM - MUMBAI

PostGIS Essentials

First published: April 2015

Production reference: 1170415

Published by Packt Publishing Ltd.
Livery Place
35 Livery Street
Birmingham B3 2PB, UK.

ISBN 978-1-78439-529-2

www.packtpub.com

Credits

Author

Angel Marquez

Reviewers

Zeeshan Chawdhary

Eric-Jan Groen

Håvard Wahl Kongsgård

Richard Zijlstra

Commissioning Editor

Pramila Balan

Acquisition Editor

James Jones

Content Development Editor

Ajinkya Paranjape

Technical Editor

Mohita Vyas

Copy Editor

Sonia Michelle Cheema

Project Coordinator

Harshal Ved

Proofreaders

Maria Gould

Joanna McMahon

Indexer

Rekha Nair

Graphics

Sheetal Aute

Jason Monteiro

Production Coordinator

Conidon Miranda

Cover Work

Conidon Miranda

About the Author

Angel Marquez is a software engineer with a master's degree in computing sciences. He has been working with GIS and open source tools for more than a decade in both public and private sectors, in his home country of Mexico.

Firstly, I would like to thank my Lord Jesus Christ, the glory is for him.

I am grateful to my wife and my little kid for being my inspiration and motivation. I would like to thank my mom, for giving me the chance of a better future, as well as my pastor Alfredo, and his wife, who always take care of their lambs. Lastly, I am thankful to all the incredible members of Packt Publishing, and especially Ajinkya for his patience and guidance.

About the Reviewers

Zeeshan Chawdhary has been experimenting with location-based technologies since 2007, having worked with industry leaders such as Foursquare, Google, and Yahoo! in the LBS space. He has been working with start-ups for the past few years. He has built and scaled up e-commerce, location-based services, and mobile apps for millions of users.

He is also an author and has written three books for Packt Publishing on iOS, Windows Phone, and iBooks Author, respectively. He is currently building the technical backbone for a self-drive car rental start-up in India.

> I would like to thank Packt Publishing for generously offering me books to review. They not only help me learn about new technologies but also strengthen what I already know, as well as how other programmers work.

Eric-Jan Groen started his GIS adventure when he started working at Automotive Navigation Data. They gave him the opportunity to experiment and explore the world of GIS. They gave him carte blanche and he worked on special products for them. While he worked there, Milo van der Linden was an inspiration to him from the beginning; later on, Milo left and he ventured forward on his own. With Bojan Sobocan acting as his supervisor, he initiated many projects and always found new tools and ways to complete the tasks he was given.

After proofreading a book on GeoServer and having had a good time doing it, reviewing this book was just as welcome.

Håvard Wahl Kongsgård is akin to a Swiss army knife when he's performing data exploration. He believes that he predicted events in small wars in a previous life. He's worked with everything from military projects and mine-clearing operations to epidemiology.

Currently, he's finishing a PhD in spatial epidemiology while working with a start-up.

Richard Zijlstra is a civil engineer with technical planning and GeoICT in general. He has used his engineering degree in The Netherlands to work on projects related to water management, infrastructure planning, and geographical information management as well as with earthquakes in Greece (Patras), all of which have an effect on environmental and social aspects. He collaborates system architecture, requirement management, and the development of geographical information technology.

At the moment, he is involved in developing an Enterprise Geo Data Architecture to store open data on earthquakes, safety, and gas exploration in the Groningen province of the northern part of The Netherlands. The project group is being set up together by University of Groningen with Geodienst at `@CIT_RUG`. Gas extraction in this area can often lead to earthquakes and also cause damage to buildings and infrastructure. The project group will set up an open geodata storage to collaborate all kinds of data, which will deal with the situation in this area.

His vision is, "Everybody uses and shares their own geographical information to share and update each other's knowledge about the physical and social environment." His mission is to find out what, where, when and why....

He is the founder and owner of Geoneer. Using his vision and point of view, he hopes that Geoneer will help and collaborate in all the aspects of geographical information technology worldwide. You can find them on Twitter at `@Geoneer` and LinkedIn at `http://www.linkedin.com/in/geoneer/`.

He has also written a lot of documents, system architectures, and about the usage of geographical information technology. The books *OpenLayers Cookbook, Packt Publishing,* and *Mastering GeoServer, Pack Publishing,* were also reviewed by him for their textual context .

I want to thank my parents for my healthy mind and the environment I grew up in as a child in the Frisian countryside. Also, I would like to thank the people of my town, Groningen, who inspired me to do a lot of things in my life. I'm very thankful to these people who have always known how I think, what I do, and what I wished to do in the future. I am extremely thankful to my son, Alessio Mori Zijlstra. He has been the greatest inspiration of my life!

www.PacktPub.com

Support files, eBooks, discount offers, and more

For support files and downloads related to your book, please visit www.PacktPub.com.

Did you know that Packt offers eBook versions of every book published, with PDF and ePub files available? You can upgrade to the eBook version at www.PacktPub.com and as a print book customer, you are entitled to a discount on the eBook copy. Get in touch with us at service@packtpub.com for more details.

At www.PacktPub.com, you can also read a collection of free technical articles, sign up for a range of free newsletters and receive exclusive discounts and offers on Packt books and eBooks.

https://www2.packtpub.com/books/subscription/packtlib

Do you need instant solutions to your IT questions? PacktLib is Packt's online digital book library. Here, you can search, access, and read Packt's entire library of books.

Why subscribe?

- Fully searchable across every book published by Packt
- Copy and paste, print, and bookmark content
- On demand and accessible via a web browser

Free access for Packt account holders

If you have an account with Packt at www.PacktPub.com, you can use this to access PacktLib today and view 9 entirely free books. Simply use your login credentials for immediate access.

Table of Contents

Preface

PostGIS is basically an extension of PostgreSQL DBMS that allows it to manage spatial datatypes. It was developed by Refractions Research Inc, a Canadian company, and published under the GNU license. Through the years, PostGIS has been observed to be a better solution than many of the other options on the market. A lot of these solutions are proprietary.

This book's objective is to be a guide for those who are new to the field of spatial databases; it covers some of the most basic and important concepts, while trying to keep them simple. At the same time, it could be useful for those of you who are advanced, have experience in this field, and are now looking for a way to graphically show the results of its spatial queries and exploit the results. This may be because you want to speed up your current queries. It might also be useful for developers who have little or no knowledge about spatial databases, but want to build desktop or web applications with spatial functionality, with only the basic concepts they have learned. This book helps you in such a way that you either go through the first chapter progressively until the end, or only focus on the chapters you're interested in without reading any of the previous ones.

This book is not a complete or exhaustive reference of PostGIS, but is more like a starting point where you will find the information that you need to start your projects, in a consolidated and easy-to-digest manner. The practical exercises will also help you brush up your knowledge along the way.

What this book covers

Chapter 1, Introducing PostGIS and Setting it Up, provides step-by-step instructions to download, install, and configure the three basic tools needed for the rest of this book: Postgres DBMS, the PostGIS extension, and QGIS for data visualization.

Chapter 2, Creating Your First Spatial Database, helps you to create your first GIS database using both the command interface and graphical tools.

Chapter 3, Inserting GIS Objects, introduces you to the basics of GIS objects and data manipulation sentences.

Chapter 4, Selecting and Filtering GIS Queries, introduces you to the making, selecting, and filtering of spatial GIS queries.

Chapter 5, Displaying GIS Data Graphically, shows you how to display query results graphically into an electronic map.

Chapter 6, Management of Vectorial and Raster Data with PostGIS, shows you how to import and export vectorial and raster data into and from a database, to and from several file formats.

Chapter 7, Performance Tuning, shows you how to speed up spatial queries by using indexes or tuning the PostgreSQL configuration for PostGIS.

Chapter 8, Developing a GIS Web Application, shows you how to create a GIS web application using open source tools.

Chapter 9, Developing a Desktop GIS Application, shows you how to create a GIS desktop application using open source tools.

What you need for this book

Basically, you will need a machine that can run Windows 7 and performs decently; 2 GB of RAM could be a good starting point. It would be desirable that you run your system on a Solid State Drive (SSD), and that you have two separate disks: one for the operating system and applications, and the other to store databases. This second disk must be bigger than the first one, depending on how much spatial data you plan to store, a 500 GB disk should be okay to do the job. If you have just one physical disk, you can make two partitions for this purpose.

Who this book is for

This book is for those of you who have little or no knowledge about spatial databases and are looking for a guide to help you explore this field in an easy and step-by-step way, through practical exercises and easy-to-understand concepts.

It will also be useful for you if you've had previous experience handling spatial databases, but also want to know about more advanced topics, such as spatial data visualization, or how to work with raster and vectorial data.

This book is a good option for developers who need to build desktop or web applications and are probably not very familiar with the spatial database approach. This book will provide you with the basics of the spatial theory and PostGIS management, so that you can rapidly start to work on your projects.

Conventions

In this book, you will find a number of text styles that distinguish between different kinds of information. Here are some examples of these styles and an explanation of their meaning.

Code words in text, database table names, folder names, filenames, file extensions, pathnames, dummy URLs, user input, and Twitter handles are shown as follows: "When the download finishes, we will get the `postgresql-9.3.x-x-windows-x64.exe` file; this is the PostgreSQL installer for our operating system."

A block of code is set as follows:

```
CREATE TABLE tbl_properties
(
town character(30),
postal_code character(10),
street character(30),
"number" integer,
the_geom geometry
);
```

Any command-line input or output is written as follows:

```
BEGIN;
CREATE TABLE "overview" ("rid" serial PRIMARY KEY,"rast"
 raster,"filename" text);
INSERT INTO "overview" ("rast","filename") VALUES
('0100000300000000000407F400300000000407FC0FFFFF
FFF2BD423C102000000161F364100000000000000000000000
0000000008… 9E9E9E9EA'::raster,'GBOverview.tif');
END;
```

New terms and **important words** are shown in bold. Words that you see on the screen, for example, in menus or dialog boxes, appear in the text like this: "Navigate to the **Database | DBManager**."

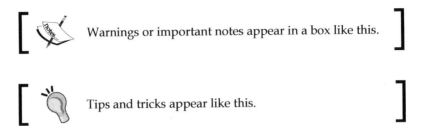

Warnings or important notes appear in a box like this.

Tips and tricks appear like this.

Reader feedback

Feedback from our readers is always welcome. Let us know what you think about this book—what you liked or disliked. Reader feedback is important for us as it helps us develop titles that you will really get the most out of.

To send us general feedback, simply e-mail feedback@packtpub.com, and mention the book's title in the subject of your message.

If there is a topic that you have expertise in and you are interested in either writing or contributing to a book, see our author guide at www.packtpub.com/authors.

Customer support

Now that you are the proud owner of a Packt book, we have a number of things to help you to get the most from your purchase.

Downloading the example code

You can download the example code files from your account at http://www.packtpub.com for all the Packt Publishing books you have purchased. If you purchased this book elsewhere, you can visit http://www.packtpub.com/support and register to have the files e-mailed directly to you.

Downloading the color images of this book

We also provide you with a PDF file that has color images of the screenshots/diagrams used in this book. The color images will help you better understand the changes in the output. You can download this file from https://www.packtpub.com/sites/default/files/downloads/52920S.pdf.

Errata

Although we have taken every care to ensure the accuracy of our content, mistakes do happen. If you find a mistake in one of our books—maybe a mistake in the text or the code—we would be grateful if you could report this to us. By doing so, you can save other readers from frustration and help us improve subsequent versions of this book. If you find any errata, please report them by visiting http://www.packtpub.com/submit-errata, selecting your book, clicking on the **Errata Submission Form** link, and entering the details of your errata. Once your errata are verified, your submission will be accepted and the errata will be uploaded to our website or added to any list of existing errata under the Errata section of that title.

To view the previously submitted errata, go to https://www.packtpub.com/books/content/support and enter the name of the book in the search field. The required information will appear under the **Errata** section.

Piracy

Piracy of copyrighted material on the Internet is an ongoing problem across all media. At Packt, we take the protection of our copyright and licenses very seriously. If you come across any illegal copies of our works in any form on the Internet, please provide us with the location address or website name immediately so that we can pursue a remedy.

Please contact us at copyright@packtpub.com with a link to the suspected pirated material.

We appreciate your help in protecting our authors and our ability to bring you valuable content.

Questions

If you have a problem with any aspect of this book, you can contact us at questions@packtpub.com, and we will do our best to address the problem.

1
Introducing PostGIS and Setting it Up

PostGIS is a powerful open source tool that allows us to develop robust spatial databases. In this chapter, we will learn some useful basic concepts through practical examples. We will also set up our working environment so we can get started with it quickly. However, before we can continue, let me tell you about a very important concept that we need to fully understand first: what is a GIS application?

Geographic Information Systems (GIS) are systems that were designed to manage and analyze spatial data, showing it to the user in a graphical way; the main aspects of a GIS system are as follows:

- **It represents spatial data as a set of layers**: A GIS application groups data of the same kind (streets, landmarks, and so on) on layers. These layers are shown to the user one above the other, thereby creating a unified view of the data. The following image shows an example of how these layers are displayed:

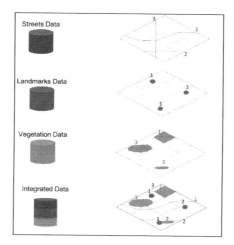

We now have an integrated view of the data, so the user can extract information generated by the combination of them; as an example, using this integrated view, we can measure the distance between the landmark 1 and the vegetation area 2.

- **It shows the spatial data above a map**: This helps users to get a better understanding of the displayed data, putting it in the context of the area of interest.

- **It has a comprehensive set of analytic and data transformation tools**: As mentioned in the last example, a GIS application must give users a way to analyze, process, and transform such spatial data, so they can get new information from the input data.

It is quite likely that you have experience and some basic knowledge of relational databases and computer programming. It will also be desirable if you have basic knowledge about geography, but if you don't, then there's no need to worry; one of this book's objectives is to explain to you some of the most important and useful concepts of geography in a practical and simplified way, so that you can understand them through the development of the book, and focus on the practical application of them. This book will also show you how powerful PostGIS can be and how much it can help you in creating strong and sometimes complex databases. By the end of the book, you should be able to develop amazing spatial projects.

In this chapter, we will cover the following topics:

- Learning about some basic GIS concepts
- Setting up the PostgreSQL database manager
- Setting up the PostGIS spatial extension
- Setting up the QGIS spatial data viewer

What is PostGIS?

PostGIS is the geographic extension of the database management system, **PostgreSQL**, which allows us to store geographic objects as part of our data tables. A geographic object is a special type of data that allows us to store a geographic position or a set of them as part of a line or a polygon. Essentially, PostGIS is a powerful tool that enables you to handle complex geographical data and visually explore this data when you use it along with graphical tools, such as QGIS.

Why PostGIS?

PostGIS is an extension of the powerful PostgreSQL, one of the most reliable open source DBMS available, which has spent a lot of time on the market, but what makes it such a good platform for PostGIS is the fact that it implements something called **Generic Index Structure** (GIST), which allows it to build indexes in almost any kind of data type. Given this flexibility and the fact that the structure of PostgreSQL gives you the chance to build custom functions very tightly to the core, PostGIS could by developed in a natural way. This is because it basically adds spatial data, spatial indexes, and spatial functions to the existing features of PostgreSQL without any complicated, intermediate, or special conversion processes. The other important features of it are:

- It has a lot, and I mean a lot, of useful spatial functions to search, analyze, convert, and manage spatial data

- It has both vectorial and raster data support; these data types will be described in *Chapter 6, Management of Vectorial and Raster Data with PostGIS*

- It's based on open standards as defined by the Open Geospatial Consortium. You can visit http://www.osgeo.org/ to know more

- For the last decade, PostGIS has been used, proved, and improved by a lot of public and private organizations all around the world

- It's supported by other well-proven open source projects (such as Proj4, GEOS, and GDAL)

- Almost all (if not all), both open and closed GIS software, have compatibility with it (such as ETL and desktop and server Geotracks)

With a GIS database, we can handle geographic data more efficiently because it contains functions and algorithms that make it easier to manipulate and analyze it.

We might come across a hypothetical situation where we are the IT department of a real estate company, and are required to develop a computational system to control the data of the houses it's selling. Currently, the company only has an electronic sheet where all this data is stored. The sheet looks similar to the following table:

Town	Postal code	Street	Number
London	N7 6PA	Holloway Road	32
West Berkshire	RG12 1DF	Charles Square	45
Bristol	BS1 4UZ	St Augustine's Parade	39

Additionally, the company wants to be able to show the geographic position of every property it has assigned on a map via its website. Suppose we don't know anything about spatial databases, we have a tight schedule, and we just want to use a traditional relational approach. The first thing we could do is to build a data table, taking the electronic sheet as a base, and adding two more fields. These fields will be doubles and will store the latitude and longitude values of the geographical position of every property. That table must be created through a command as shown in the following code snippet:

```
CREATE TABLE tbl_properties
(
town character(30),
postal_code character(10),
street character(30),
"number" integer,
latitude double precision,
longitude double precision
);
```

In *Chapter 2, Creating Your First Spatial Database*, we will see how to run these kinds of commands. The created table must look similar to the following table:

Town	Postal code	Street	Number	Latitude	Longitude
London	N7 6PA	Holloway Road	32	51.556173	-0.116190
West Berkshire	RG12 1DF	Charles Square	45	51.381320	-1.344165
Bristol	BS1 4UZ	St Augustine's Parade	39	51.453462	-2.598348

Has the problem been solved or not? What if our boss wants to know which houses are located at least 10 miles away from the local supermarket of some specific town? Well, we could develop a software in our favorite programming language that reads the position of every house in the table and calculates the distance between the supermarket and the house. The main problem with this approach is that we have to write our own function to calculate the distance, but these functions can have errors that show us the wrong results. Another problem here is the fact that when we need to run a radius-based search (looking for all the objects located at *x* distance from a specific position), we will need to go through the entire table, making comparisons with every register; there is no way to use an optimization mechanism as an index to hasten the query.

If, instead of doing this, we use a geographical field to store these positions, we will only have to make a spatial query to achieve the result we're looking for. Here is an example of how we could create our table with the spatial field instead of the doubles:

```
CREATE TABLE tbl_properties
(
town character(30),
postal_code character(10),
street character(30),
"number" integer,
the_geom geometry
);
```

Now, in order to insert the spatial data into the table we must use the following query:

```
INSERT INTO tbl_properties (town, postal_code, street, "number", the_
geom) VALUES ('London', 'N7 6PA', 'Holloway Road', 32, ST_GeomFromEWKT
('SRID=4326;POINT(-0.116190, 51.556173)'));
```

The result will be similar to the following:

Town	Postal code	Street	Number	the_geom
London	N7 6PA	Holloway Road	32	POINT(-0.116190, 51.556173)
West Berkshire	RG12 1DF	Charles Square	45	POINT(-1.344165, 51.381320)
Bristol	BS1 4UZ	St Augustine's Parade	39	POINT(-2.598348, 51.453462)

The following query asks the database to bring all the registers that are located at 10 statute miles (the distance, in this case, must be given in degrees, so, we have divided 10 miles by 69.047, the equivalent of one degree in statute miles) from the geographical position where the latitude is 51.56 and the longitude is -0.117. Supposing that this is the geographic position of our fictitious supermarket, this position is stored and is a point geometry object on the database:

```
SELECT * FROM tbl_properties WHERE ST_DWithin(the_geom, ST_
GeomFromText('POINT(-0.117, 51.56)',4326), (10.0 / 69.047) );
```

In the following chapters, we will explain how to make spatial queries. This is an example of exactly how useful spatial databases can be; taking some time to understand how to use them will certainly be useful.

Before we can start working on spatial databases, we have to prepare our working environment. In the following sections of this chapter, we will see how to do this step by step.

Installing PostgreSQL

PostgreSQL is a powerful **Object-Relational Database Management System (ORDBMS)**. We need this because PostGIS is just an extension of it. It's open source and free of cost.

The first thing we have to do is download and install the PostgreSQL database management system. In this book, we will assume that you are working on a 64-bit Windows machine with a version of Windows 7 or later. We will use the most recent stable version available at the time of the writing, which is the Version 9.3. Perform the following steps:

1. First, we have to navigate to the official site, `http://www.postgresql.org`.

2. Then, we have to go to the **Download** section at `http://www.postgresql.org/download/`, as shown in the following screenshot:

Downloads

PostgreSQL Core Distribution

The core of the PostgreSQL object-relational database management system is available in several source and binary formats.

Binary packages

Pre-built binary packages are available for a number of different operating systems:

- BSD
  - FreeBSD
  - OpenBSD
- Linux
  - Red Hat family Linux (including CentOS/Fedora/Scientific/Oracle variants)
  - Debian GNU/Linux and derivatives
  - Ubuntu Linux and derivatives
  - SuSE and OpenSuSE
  - Other Linux
- Mac OS X
- Solaris
- Windows

3. After this, we need to go to the **Binary packages** section of the page and select the **Windows** hyperlink:

> **Windows installers**
>
> **Graphical installer**
>
> The graphical installer for PostgreSQL includes the PostgreSQL server, pgAdmin III; a graphical tool for managing and developing your databases, and StackBuilder; a package manager that can be used to download and install additional PostgreSQL applications and drivers.
>
> The installer is designed to be as straightforward as possible and the fastest way to get up and running with PostgreSQL on Windows.
>
> Download the installer from EnterpriseDB for all supported versions.
>
> *Advanced users* can also download a zip archive of the binaries, without the installer. This is not recommended for normal installations, it is intended for users who wish to include PostgreSQL as part of another application installer.

4. Now, we have to choose the download hyperlink in the paragraph **Download the installer from EnterpriseDB for all supported versions.** as shown in the preceding screenshot.

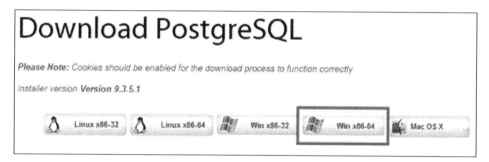

5. Similar to the preceding screenshot, we will select the most recent stable version and the **Win 86-64** installer.

6. When the download finishes, we will get the `postgresql-9.3.x-x-windows-x64.exe` file; this is the PostgreSQL installer for our operating system. Now, we will double-click on this file.

7. Immediately, we can see a dialog box where the operating system asks us for permission to run this file. We must allow this file to be executed as a system manager, as shown in the following screenshot:

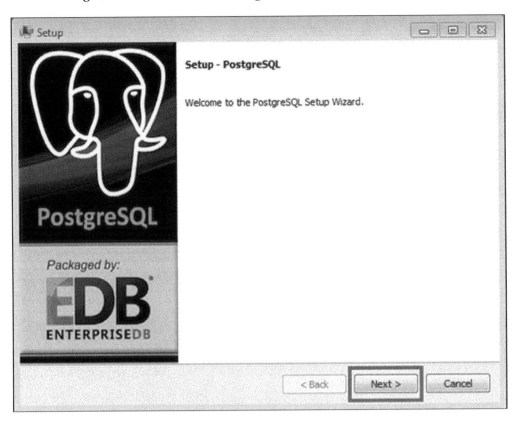

8. We will choose an installation folder, or just leave the default one (C:\Program Files\PostgreSQL\9.3), and click on the **Next** button.

9. Next, we need to select a folder where all the data of our databases will be installed. You can just select the default (C:\Program Files\ PostgreSQL\9.3\data), but it would be very desirable to select a folder from another partition different from the one that uses the operating system; this can help you to avoid losing your data if you have to format your system for any reason.

10. We will see a screen with two text areas where we will need to type and retype a password for the Postgres user. This password can be anything that you want, but it cannot be an empty string. Be careful with the password you choose because if you forget it, there is no way to get it back; we will have to reinstall everything again!

11. Now, we have to choose a listening port.

12. Then, we will see a dialog screen that asks you to select a **Regional Configuration**. We can leave the default option, which means the same language configuration that you have on your operating system, and then click on the **Next** button.

13. Once the installer has finished copying the files, it will show a screen that will tell you that the installation of PostgreSQL has finished. Here is something important to keep in mind: the screen has a checkbox inside that asks you whether you want to execute the Stack Builder at the end of the installation. At this moment, we will choose not to do so. This checkbox must be unchecked. In the next section of this chapter, we will properly explain what the Stack Builder is, and what it is for. Now, we can click the **Finish** button.

14. Finally, PosgreSQL is installed on your machine. You can check whether the installation was successful by executing a graphical tool for the DBMS called PGAdmin III. Then you will see the main window. On the left-hand side is the list of servers; in this case we just have one server:

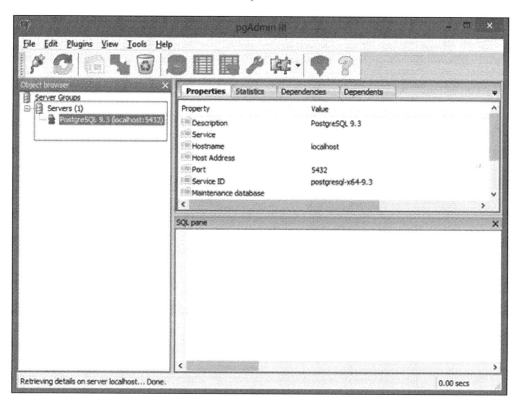

15. Double-click on the **PostgreSQL 9.3 (localhost 5432)** server and a dialog box called **Connect to Server** will be shown. In this box, you must type your Postgres user password and click on the **OK** button. If you wish, you can check the **Store password** checkbox; it stores your password in this machine so you don't have to type it every time you log in to your database:

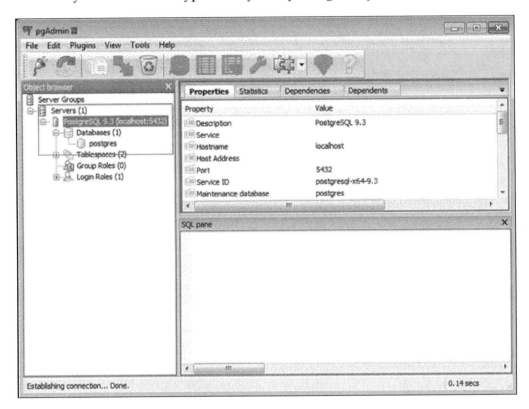

Installing PostGIS

In the previous section of this chapter, we mentioned the Stack Builder; it's an application that allows us to install several additional options or extensions for PostgreSQL. Using this tool, we will install PostGIS in our database server. The following procedure applies even if you have previously installed a version of PostgreSQL higher than 8.X:

1. First, you have to execute the application Stack Builder tool installed with PostgreSQL.

2. We will see a dialog box that asks us for permission to execute this app, you have to click on the **Yes** button.

3. Now, you can see a window with a combo box in the center, where you have to choose the server that you want to configure. In this case, we only have one installed in our computer; you must select the **PostgreSQL 9.3 (x64) on port 5432** option and click on the **Next** button:

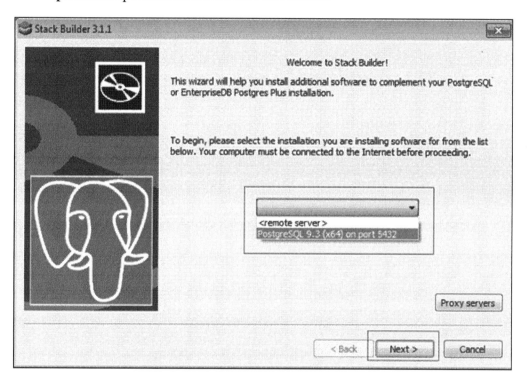

4. Next, we will see the same window as before, but with a list of available applications for installation grouped by categories; we will select the **Spatial Extensions** category:

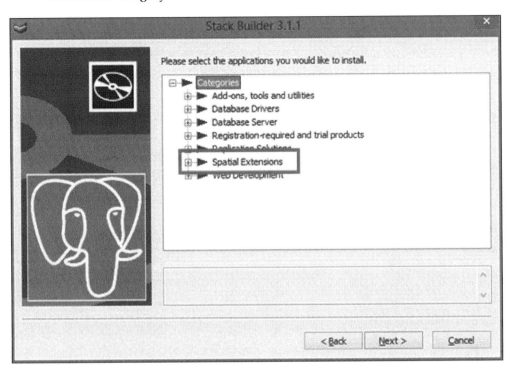

5. Now, you must click on **PostGIS 2.1 Bundle for PostgreSQL 9.3 (64 bit) v2.1.x** and click on the **Next** button.

6. Then, you will see a window that shows the packages you have selected. In another area positioned after that, we can select a folder where all the required files will be downloaded. This is *not* the installation folder; if you don't have any trouble with the default directory, you can click on the **Next** button.

7. When it finishes, you will see a window telling you that the application has downloaded the required file and it can start to install it in your computer. Leave the **Skip Installation** checkbox unchecked and click on the **Next** button:

All the installation files have now been successfully downloaded.

Please click the "Next" button to start the installations.

Note: You must allow all installations to run to completion. If you are prompted to restart the computer, click "No" or "Restart Later" and manually restart your computer when all the installation have finished.

☐ Skip Installation

[< Back] [Next >] [Cancel]

8. Now, you can see another window that shows the license agreement. It's not necessary that you read the entire document; you can to click the **I Agree** button.

9. Once you have done this, you will see a window that shows the components that need to be selected and installed. In the middle, it has a checkbox, where **PostGIS** is checked, and another with the text, **Create spatial database**, which is unchecked. Check this one and click on the **Next** button:

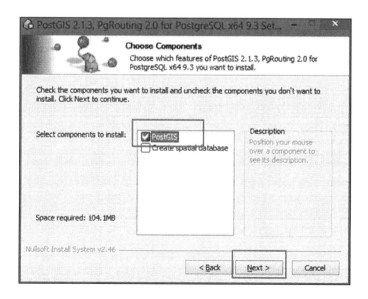

10. Now, you have to choose a destination folder for the installation; you can leave the default one and click on the **Next** button.

11. Then, a window appears where you have to log in to the database. Just type your Postgres user password, defined in the previous section, and click on the **Next** button.

12. In the next window, you will have to add a name for your spatial database. In this case, I named it spatial_db1, but you can name it whatever you want; type the name and click on the **Install** button, as shown in the following screenshot:

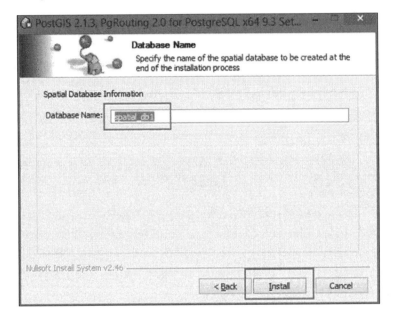

13. Next, it will show you a dialog box that asks you for permission to set the GDAL_DATA environment variable. At this moment, I will only tell you that GDAL is a very useful and important library that PostGIS uses internally. You have to click on the **Yes** button:

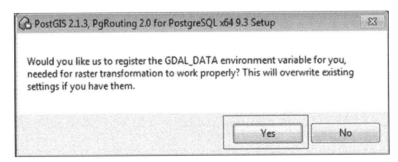

14. Now another dialog box appears, asking you to decide whether you want to set the `POSTGIS_GDAL_ENABLED_DRIVERS`; you will have to click on the **Yes** button. In later chapters, I will tell you more about these system variables:

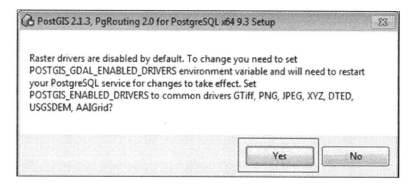

15. Another dialog box appears, asking you for permission to set `POSTGIS_ENABLE_OUTDB_RASTERS`; click on the **Yes** button, as shown in the following screenshot. We will see what a raster data is in *Chapter 6, Management of Vectorial and Raster Data with PostGIS*:

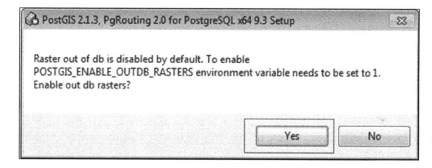

16. Lastly, the installer shows a window that tells you that the installation is completed. Now you just have to click on the **Close** button.

17. Now, maximize the **Application Stack Builder** window and click on the **Finish** button.

Congratulations!, Now you have PostgreSQL with the PostGIS extension installed on your machine. You can check whether everything is okay by running PGAdmin III, and then running the following query in the Postgres database:

```
SELECT name, default_version,installed_version  FROM pg_available_
extensions WHERE name LIKE 'postgis%' ;
```

You must get a result dataset as shown in the following table:

name	default_version	installed_version
postgis	2.1.5	
Postgis tiger geocoder	2.1.5	
Postgis topology	2.1.5	

This means that you have the PostGIS extension available on your database server and you can include it in any new databases that you create.

Finally, we will install the QGIS application. It's an open source project that allows us to graphically represent the geographical data stored in several formats, including the data that is stored in our database.

Installing QGIS

QGIS is a free and open source geographic information system. It's very user friendly and it can read a lot of spatial formats, and it's an excellent tool for seeing the data we generated graphically. You can visit the project's official site at `http://www.qgis.org/en/site/`. Perform the following steps for the installation:

1. For installation, go to the project website in the **For Users** section at `http://www.qgis.org/en/site/forusers/index.html`.

2. Then, you have to click on the **Download QGIS** button.

3. You will need to select the Windows version section. Once inside the section, you will find a **QGIS standalone Installer Version 2.4 (64-bit)** link; click on it.

4. The installer will start to download; when it finishes, you need to double-click on the file for the installation to begin.

5. Then, you will see a welcome window; click on the **Next** button:

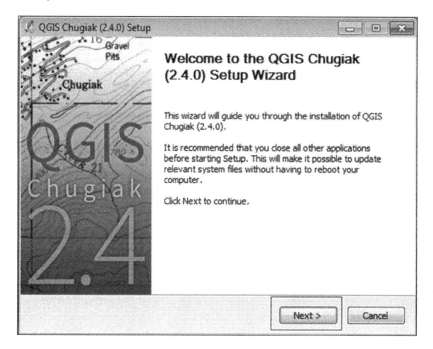

6. After this, you will see a window with the agreement license; click on the **I accept** button.

7. Then, select a destination folder for the installation. You can just leave the default and click on the **Next** button. The installation requires 1.2 GB of disk free space; make sure that you have it in your disk partition.

8. Now, you can select which components will be installed. By default, the **QGIS** option is selected; leave it the way it is, and click on the **Install** button:

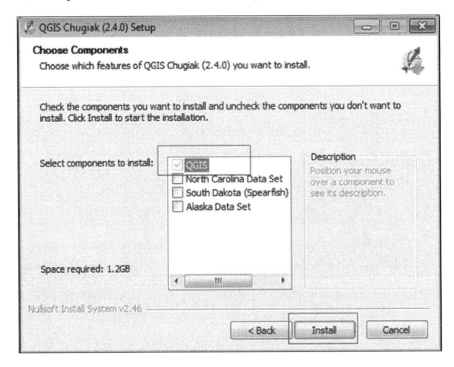

9. When it finishes, the installation will be complete and you will see a window that confirms it; now just click on the **Finish** button.

10. Once QGIS is installed, we can execute the QGIS Desktop 2.4.0 application. If the application was correctly installed, you will see the following window:

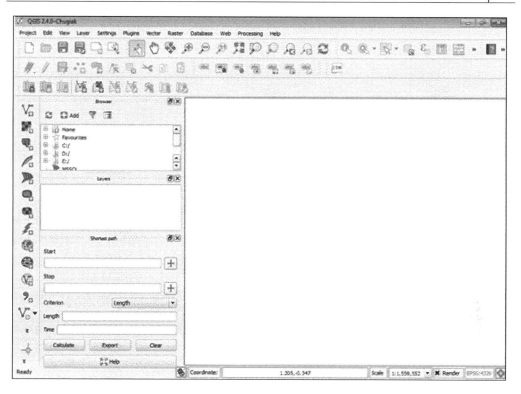

Summary

At this moment, we have learned how to install and set up our working environment in order to use the PostGIS extension, and through this we have also learned some useful geographic concepts that will allow you to get a better understanding of how PostGIS works. So, we have installed the QGIS application that will allow us to graphically explore our databases and check that everything is okay with the data.

Now, we are ready to start developing our first spatial database, for this we will continue with a practical example at the beginning of the next chapter.

2
Creating Your First Spatial Database

Now that we have installed PostgreSQL with the PostGIS extension, we are ready to develop our first spatial database. Remember that a spatial database is the one that allows us to create geometric fields to store the geographic data (points, lines, or polygons) that will represent the real life data. This way we will be able to use all the advantages that PostGIS gives to spatial data management.

We will continue the real estate company example of the previous chapter; we will explain how to develop the necessary databases and data tables using both the command line and graphical tools available. In this chapter, we will cover the following topics:

- Create spatial databases via a command line and GUI
- Create tables with spatial fields via a command line, GUI, and SQL scripts

The development of spatial databases

After an extensive analysis of the company's situation, the IT Department have deployed a solution, which consists of making two databases:

- The first one will carry all the corporative information, including the data of the properties for sale along with its spatial position.

- The second one will be a larger database that will store geographic data of the different cities where the company have properties for sale. These features will include: buildings, highways, landmarks, and so on and will be accessed less often.

The use of two separate databases could add more complexity to the following examples, but this is exactly what we are looking for. In the following chapters, we will see how we could work with two databases at the same time, and how we can develop queries that use data from both the databases. The idea is that you will be able to manage this situation if you find it in the real world. In the next chapter, we will see how to obtain the data and fill it with the second database.

Creating our first database using a command line

Well, it's time to create our first spatial database; PostGIS offers us several ways to do it, graphical or via a command line. In this section, you will see both of them and you will be able to select the one that you like more. There is nothing special about any of them, because the final result is the same for both of them.

Before we can start to develop the first database, we have to make executable binaries of PostgreSQL visible to our operative system, in this case Windows 7. For this, we will include the application's path to the PATH system variable. Perform the following steps:

1. First, navigate to **Start | Control Panel | System and Security | System**.
2. After that click the **Advanced system settings** option.
3. There, click the **Advanced** tab and click the **Environment variables** button.
4. Then, select the **System Variables grid** and select the row with the **Path** value on the **Variable** field.

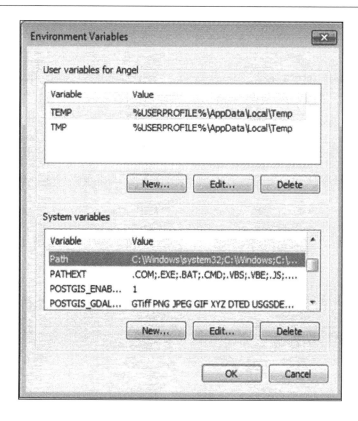

5. Once this row is selected, click on the **Edit** button.

6. A window named **Edit System Variable** will show up. Edit the **Variable value:** field by adding the following line at the end: ;C:\Program Files\ PostgreSQL\9.3\bin.

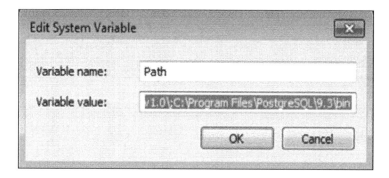

7. Click the **OK** button in all the opened windows to save the changes.

8. Restart your computer for the changes to take effect.

Now we can start to build the first spatial database using the command line, by following the next series of steps:

1. For creating the database, click on the **Start** button and type in the **Search programs and files** section cmd. Then, you will see the system's prompt. We will call our first database Real-State, so we will type the appropriate command for building it up. In the command prompt, we will type the following:

   ```
   createdb -U postgres Real-State
   ```

   Here, the -U parameter indicates the name of the user who will own the database. After that, execute this command as the database has to be created:

   ```
   Microsoft Windows [Version 6.1.7600]
   Copyright (c) 2009 Microsoft Corporation.  All rights reserved.

   C:\Users\Angel>createdb -U postgres Real-State_
   ```

2. To select the database, in the same window, type the following command:

   ```
   psql -d Real-State -U postgres
   ```

   If the system asks you for a password, type the Postgres user password. With this command, you are selecting the Real-State database to start to work with it:

   ```
   C:\Users\Angel>psql -d Real-State -U postgres
   psql (9.3.5)
   WARNING: Console code page (850) differs from Windows code page (1252)
            8-bit characters might not work correctly. See psql reference
            page "Notes for Windows users" for details.
   Type "help" for help.

   Real-State=#  _
   ```

3. As you can see, we are getting a warning message from the console. This message tells us that the character code of the application differs from the rest of the operating system; this could cause problems with 8-bit characters within psql. To avoid this problem, we must type the following command before we start working with psql:

   ```
   cmd.exe /c chcp 1252
   ```

4. We are changing the default character set of the operating system to be the same as that of psql. This change will take effect just in the present session. You will have to type this every time you open a new `cmd` window for work with your database in text mode. You can also create a batch file to run this command before you start to work with psql; just type the previous command on notepad and save it with the `.bat` extension:

```
C:\Users\Angel>cmd.exe /c chcp 1252
Active code page: 1252

C:\Users\Angel>psql -d Real-State -U postgres
psql (9.3.5)
Type "help" for help.

Real-State=#
```

5. For creating the spatial extension, we will turn our database into a spatial one with spatial functions and analyze options on your data, by executing the following command in the psql prompt:

    CREATE EXTENSION postgis;

6. After that, we will see that the command prompt responds showing us CREATE EXTENSION in the console; this tells us that the commands were executed successfully.

```
Real-State=# CREATE EXTENSION postgis;
CREATE EXTENSION
Real-State=#
```

Creating our first spatial data table using a command line

Before we can continue, it is necessary to explain a spatial table. Well, a spatial table has a field of a special type called geometry; this is the data type that allows us to store geographic data and it's only available after the spatial extension is created in our database. There is another geographic data type called *geography*, it's mainly used in order to get more accuracy in long distance measurements; the problem here is that it uses more complex mathematics and there are less spatial functions that accept this data type as a parameter. For our example, the geometric field will be called `the_geom` in every spatial table we make.

Now that the database is created, we can start to create our first spatial table. We will call it `tbl_properties` and it will store the information about the properties that the company has in consignment for sale. For this, you will have to type the following lines in the psql command prompt:

```
CREATE TABLE tbl_properties
  ( id integer NOT NULL,
town character(30),
postal_code character(10),
street character(30),
"number" integer,
the_geom geometry,
CONSTRAINT pk_id PRIMARY KEY (id)
);
```

You have to type every line with an *Enter* at the end. When you type the ; character before the *Enter* key, you are telling the command line interpreter (psql) that this is where the instruction ends and it has to execute it, as shown in the following screenshot:

As in the past executions, the command line interpreter echoes us the name of the last command that was successfully executed. In this case, we have to see the CREATE TABLE string in the command prompt.

Creating a spatial database using GUI

There are a lot of people who prefer to use the command line instead of a graphical GUI for interacting with the DBMS. If you are not one of them, you can make all these operations using the PGAdmin application. Now, we will create another database called `Real-World` that will store geographic features of the cities where the company have properties for sale:

1. First, we will click the windows **Start** button and type `pgadmin` in the **Search programs and files** text box. After that, we will execute the PGAdmin III application.

2. Once the main window is shown, we must double-click on the **PostgreSQL 9.3 (localhost:5432)** icon for opening the local server, as shown in the following screenshot:

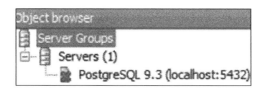

3. Once it's opened, we have to click the **Databases** item that belongs to the local server. Then, we have to right-click in this item and it will show a pop-up menu with three options, you will have to choose the **New Database** option:

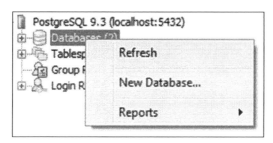

4. There, you will see a **New Database...** window; there, in the **Properties** tab, you can set the database name by typing `Real-World` in the **Name** text box. In the **Owner** combo box, select the **postgres** user, as shown in the following screenshot:

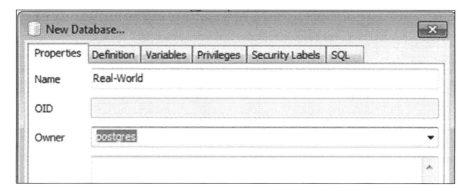

5. After that, navigate to **Definition | Template**. You will see a list of the available databases in your server. Select the **Real-Estate** database as a template, before we can do it, the template database must be closed, if it is not, you have to right-click on it and select the option **Disconnect Database**. After that, click the **OK** button for the changes to take effect.

We have used this database as a template instead of creating a new one from scratch; this technique could be useful if you need to create a new database with the same structure of an existing one (maybe for testing).

Creating a spatial data table using GUI

Now you have a second database called Real-World, let's expand it and see all the items that are inside of it:

- **Catalogs**: Here is where PostgreSQL stores information about tables and columns that conforms the database itself. As an example, when you create a new table, the information about it and its columns are stored there in the form of registers of system tables.

- **Event Triggers**: Those are procedures defined by the user that can be written in most of the available procedural languages as PL/pgSQL, PL/Tcl, PL/Perl, and PL/Python, that PostgreSQL will run when a certain event, defined by the user, fires up.

- **Extensions**: These are data structures, data types, functions, and so on that are defined by a third-party entity and that can be added to existing databases to extend its functionality.

- **Schemas**: A schema is a group of tables, data types, functions, and operators. A single database can have several of these schemas and their main function is to create a logical separation between objects. They are like directories on an operating system, except that they can't be nested.

- **Slony Replication**: It's the PostgreSQL master-slave replication system. It's designed to backup data online from the master database.

We will store spatial features of the cities where the company has properties for sale. We will create a set of spatial tables, the first of them called tbl_buildings and will be developed using the graphical tool. For this, you have to perform the following steps:

1. Double-click the **Real-World** database for it to open.

2. Click on the **+** symbol that is to the left of the database. You will see the list of components that integrates the database. Click in **Schemas (1)** (we have explained schemas earlier):

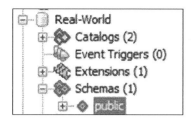

3. You will see that there is only one schema called **public**, expand it. There you will see a list of items that form the schema. A database can contain one or more schemas that logically group data tables, it's analogous as a directory of the operating system.

4. Right-click in the **Tables** item. There you will see a pop-up menu, select the **New Table...** option.

5. You will now see a window called **New Table...**. Here, you must specify the new table features. Type `tbl_buildings` in the **Name** text box and in the **Owner** combo box, select **postgres**.

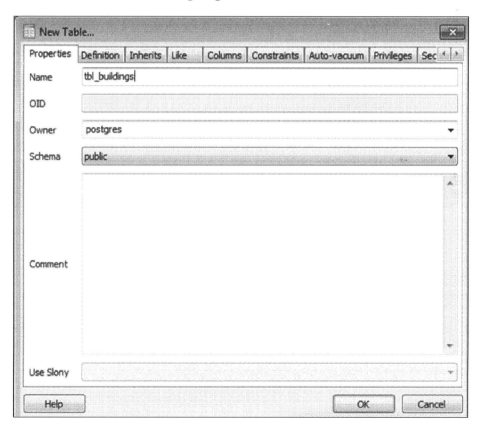

6. Now click the **Columns** tab. There you must specify the definition of every field in the table. For this click the **Add** button.

   You will see a window called **New Column**. Here we will to specify the **Name**, **data type** and **Length** if the data type is a character. You will have to do this for every field in your table. Here is a list of the required fields for this example:

Name	Data Type	Length	Description
id	character	7	Unique identifier
name	character	20	Name of the building
type	character	10	Type of building
address	character	30	Address of building
the_geom	geometry	null	Geometric representation

7. Once you have all the fields, click on the **constraints** tab, select **Primary key** (a primary key is a field that holds a value that uniquely identifies a data row) in the combo box that is in the bottom part of the window, and click on the **Add** button.

8. Then, a window called **New Primary key...** will be shown. In the **Name** text box, type pk_buildings_id without the quotes:

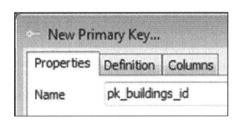

9. Then, click on the **Columns** tab. In the **Column** combo box, select **id** and click on the **add** button.

10. After that, click on the **OK** button for the changes to take effect.

Well, now that we know how to create our tables from the GUI it's time to learn a more automatic way to do it; we can develop a script and run it later. This can be very useful, if as an example, you need to create our data tables from a script generated by a database design tool. You can export the design model of your data tables to SQL scripts and run it later.

Creating a spatial data table using a SQL script

Now, we have the first table on the Real-World database. For the developing of the second table, we will follow a different method. Here, we will define the table structure using SQL language and then we will execute this script directly in the GUI. The steps we have to perform are as follows:

1. Define the table script using a simple text editor, the following is the script of the `tbl_landmarks` table:

```
CREATE TABLE tbl_landmarks
( id character(7) NOT NULL,
name character(30),
type character(15),
the_geom geometry,
CONSTRAINT pk_landmark_id PRIMARY KEY (id) );
```

2. Open the PGAdmin application and click on the **SQL** magnify glass icon:

3. There you will see an SQL query editor, copy the table script and paste it inside of the editor. Execute the query by clicking the green triangle on the tool bar.

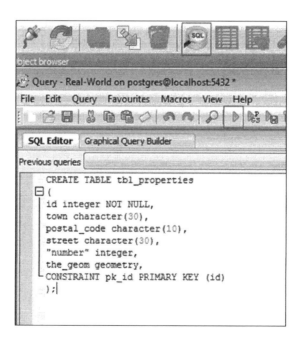

4. If the query was successfully executed, you will see the message **Query returned successfully with no result** in the **messages** tab at the bottom of the window. If instead you get an error message, check your script carefully, looking for errors.

Now that you know all the possible methods that exist for creating a spatial database in PostgreSQL, you can choose whichever of them you feel more comfortable with. The result of each one of those methods is the same for all cases.

Summary

In this chapter, you learned how to create a spatial database using both command line and the GUI, and to develop spatial tables too. It's very important that those two processes were fully understood before we can continue.

In the next chapter, we will learn how to fill those tables by obtaining the data from publicly open and freely available sources.

3

Inserting GIS Objects

Now is the time to fill our tables with data. It's very important to understand some of the theoretical concepts about spatial data before we can properly work with it. We will cover this concept through the real estate company example, used previously.

Basically, we will insert two kinds of data: firstly, all the data that belongs to our own scope of interest. By this, I mean the spatial data that was generated by us (the positions of properties in the case of the example of the real estate company) for our specific problem, so as to save this data in a way that can be easily exploited. Secondly, we will import data of a more general use, which was provided by a third party.

Another important feature that we will cover in this chapter are the spatial data files that we could use to share, import, and export spatial data within a standardized and popular format called shp or Shape files. In this chapter, we will cover the following topics:

- Developing insertion queries that include GIS objects
- Obtaining useful spatial data from a public third-party
- Filling our spatial tables with the help of spatial data files using a command line tool
- Filling our spatial tables with the help of spatial data files using a GUI tool provided by PostGIS

Developing insertion queries with GIS objects

Developing an insertion query is a very common task for someone who works with databases. Basically, we follow the SQL language syntax of the insertion, by first listing all the fields involved and then listing all the data that will be saved in each one:

```
INSERT INTO tbl_properties( id, town, postal_code, street, "number)
VALUES (1, 'London', 'N7 6PA', 'Holloway Road', 32);
```

If the field is of a numerical value, we simply write the number; if it's a string-like data type, we have to enclose the text in two single quotes.

Now, if we wish to include a spatial value in the insertion query, we must first find a way to represent this value. This is where the **Well-Known Text (WKT)** notation enters. WKT is a notation that represents a geometry object that can be easily read by humans; following is an example of this:

```
POINT(-0.116190 51.556173)
```

Here, we defined a geographic point by using a list of two real values, the latitude (y-axis) and the longitude (x-axis). Additionally, if we need to specify the elevation of some point, we will have to specify a third value for the z-axis; this value will be defined in meters by default, as shown in the following code snippet:

```
POINT(-0.116190 51.556173 100)
```

Some of the other basic geometry types defined by the WKT notation are:

- **MULTILINESTRING**: This is used to define one or more lines
- **POLYGON**: This is used to define only one polygon
- **MULTIPOLYGON**: This is used to define several polygons in the same row

So, as an example, an SQL insertion query to add the first row to the table, `tbl_properties`, of our real estate database using the WKT notation, should be as follows:

```
INSERT INTO tbl_properties (id, town, postal_code, street, "number",
the_geom) VALUES (1, 'London', 'N7 6PA', 'Holloway Road', 32, ST_
GeomFromText('POINT(-0.116190 51.556173)'));
```

The special function provided by PostGIS, `ST_GeomFromText`, parses the text given as a parameter and converts it into a GIS object that can be inserted in `the_geom` field.

Now, we could think this is everything and, therefore, start to develop all the insertion queries that we need. It could be true if we just want to work with the data generated by us and there isn't a need to share this information with other entities. However, if we want to have a better understanding of GIS (believe me, it could help you a lot and prevent a lot of unnecessary headache when working with data from several sources), it would be better to specify another piece of information as part of our GIS object representation to establish its **Spatial Reference System** (**SRS**). In the next section, we will explain this concept.

What is a spatial reference system?

We could think about Earth as a perfect sphere that will float forever in space and never change its shape, but it is not. Earth is alive and in a state of constant change, and it's certainly not a perfect circle; it is more like an ellipse (though not a perfect ellipse) with a lot of small variations, which have taken place over the years.

If we want to represent a specific position inside this irregular shape called Earth, we must first make some abstractions:

1. First we have to choose a method to represent Earth's surface into a regular form (such as a sphere, ellipsoid, and so on).

2. After this, we must take this abstract three-dimensional form and represent it into a two-dimensional plane. This process is commonly called **map projection**, also known as **projection**.

There are a lot of ways to make a projection; some of them are more precise than others. This depends on the usefulness that we want to give to the data, and the kind of projection that we choose.

The SRS defines which projection will be used and the transformation that will be used to translate a position from a given projection to another. This leads us to another important point. Maybe it has occurred to you that a geographic position was unique, but it is not. By this, I mean that there could be two different positions with the same latitude and longitude values but be in different physical places on Earth. For a position to be unique, it is necessary to specify the SRS that was used to obtain this position.

To explain this concept, let's consider Earth as a perfect sphere; how can you represent it as a two-dimensional square? Well, to do this, you will have to make a projection, as shown in the following figure:

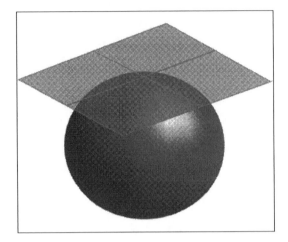

A projection implies that you will have to make a spherical 3D image fit into a 2D figure, as shown in the preceding image; there are several ways to achieve this. We applied an azimuthal projection, which is a result of projecting a spherical surface onto a plane. However, as I told you earlier, there are several other ways to do this, as we can see in the following image:

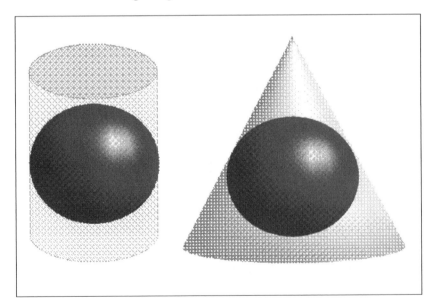

These are examples of cylindrical and conical projections. Each one produces a different kind of 2D image of the terrain. Each has its own peculiarities and is used for several distinct purposes. If we put all the resultant images of these projections one above the other, we must get an image similar to the following figure:

As you can see, the terrain positions, which are not necessary, are the same between two projections, so you must clearly specify which projection you are using in your project in order to avoid possible mistakes and errors when you establish a position.

There are a lot of SRS defined around the world. They could be grouped by their reach, that is, they could be local (state or province), national (an entire country), regional (several countries from the same area), or global (worldwide). The International Association of Oil and Gas Producers has defined a collection of **Coordinate Reference System (CRS)** known as the **European Petroleum Survey Group (EPSG)** dataset and has assigned a unique ID to each of these SRSs; this ID is called SRID.

For uniquely defining a position, you must establish the SRS that it belongs to, using its particular ID; this is the SRID. There are literally hundreds of SRSs defined; to avoid any possible error, we must standardize which SRS we will use. A very common SRS, widely used around the globe and the one that we will use in this book, is the WGS84 SRS with the SRID 4326. It is very important that you store the spatial data on your database, using EPSG: 4326 as much as possible, or almost use one equal projection on your database; this way you will avoid problems when you analyze your data.

The WKT notation doesn't support the SRID specification as part of the text, since this was developed at the EWKT notation that allows us to include this information as part of our input string, as we will see in the following example:

```
'SRID=4326;POINT(51.556173 -0.116190)'
```

When you create a spatial field, you must specify the SRID that will be used. In the previous chapter, we didn't specify this. When you do this, all the SRIDs will be set to -1. I would recommend that you create your spatial field, specifying the data from the beginning. Now that the concept of an SRS has been established, we will be able to go back and correct the tables that we developed in the previous chapter.

Including SRS information in our spatial tables

The matter that was discussed in the previous section is very important to develop our spatial tables. Taking into account the SRS that they will use from the beginning, we will follow a procedure to recreate our tables by adding this feature. This procedure must be applied to all the tables that we have created on both databases. Perform the following steps:

1. Open a command session on pgSQL in your command line tool or by using the graphical GUI, PGAdmin III. We will open the `Real_Estate` database.

2. Drop the spatial fields of your tables using the following instruction:

    ```
    SELECT DropGeometryColumn('tbl_properties', 'the_geom') Add the
    spatial field using this command:
    SELECT AddGeometryColumn('tbl_properties', 'the_geom', 4326,
    'POINT', 2);
    ```

    Repeat these steps for the rest of the spatial tables.

3. Now that we can specify the SRS that was used to obtain this position, we will develop an insertion query using the **Extended WKT (EWKT)** notation:

    ```
    INSERT INTO tbl_properties ( id, town, postal_code, street,
    "number", the_geom)VALUES (1, 'London', 'N7 6PA', 'Holloway Road',
    32, ST_GeomFromEWKT('SRID=4326;POINT(51.556173 -0.116190)'));
    ```

The ST_GeomFromEWKT function works exactly as ST_GeomFromText, but it implements the extended functionality of the WKT notation. Now that you know how to represent a GIS object as text, it is up to you to choose the most convenient way to generate a SQL script that inserts existing data into the spatial data tables. As an example, you could develop a macro in Excel, a desktop application in C#, a PHP script on your server, and so on.

Getting data from external sources

In this section, we will learn how to obtain data from third-party sources. Most often, this data interchange is achieved through a spatial data file. There are many data formats for this file (such as KML, geoJSON, and so on). We will choose to work with the *.shp files, because they are widely used and supported in practically all the GIS tools available in the market.

There are dozens of sites where you could get useful spatial data from practically any city, state, or country in the world. Much of this data is public and freely available. In this case, we will use data from a fabulous website called http://www.openstreetmap.org/.

The following is a series of steps that you could follow if you want to obtain spatial data from this particular provider. I'm pretty sure you can easily adapt this procedure to obtain data from another provider on the Internet. Using the example of the real estate company, we will get data from the English county of Buckinghamshire. The idea is that you, as a member of the IT department, import data from the cities where the company has activities:

1. Open your favorite Internet browser and go to http://www.openstreetmap.org/, as shown in the following screenshot:

2. Click on the **Export** tab.

3. Click on the **Geofabrik Downloads** link; you will be taken to `http://download.geofabrik.de/`, as shown in the following screenshot:

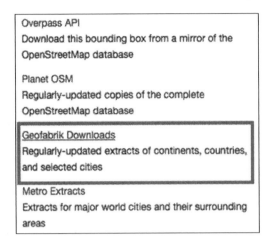

Overpass API
Download this bounding box from a mirror of the OpenStreetMap database

Planet OSM
Regularly-updated copies of the complete OpenStreetMap database

Geofabrik Downloads
Regularly-updated extracts of continents, countries, and selected cities

Metro Extracts
Extracts for major world cities and their surrounding areas

4. There, you will find a list of sub regions of the world; select **Europe**:

Sub-Region	Quick Links		
	.osm.pbf	.shp.zip	.osm.bz2
Africa	[.osm.pbf]	✗	[.osm.bz2]
Antarctica	[.osm.pbf]	[.shp.zip]	[.osm.bz2]
Asia	[.osm.pbf]	✗	[.osm.bz2]
Australia and Oceania	[.osm.pbf]	✗	[.osm.bz2]
Central America	[.osm.pbf]	✗	[.osm.bz2]
Europe	[.osm.pbf]	✗	[.osm.bz2]
North America	[.osm.pbf]	✗	[.osm.bz2]
South America	[.osm.pbf]	✗	[.osm.bz2]

5. Next is a list of all countries in Europe; notice a new column called **.shp.zip**. This is the file format that we need to download. Select **Great Britain**:

Georgia (Eastern Europe)	[.osm.pbf] (27.6 MB)	[.shp.zip]	[.osm.bz2]
Germany	[.osm.pbf] (2.2 GB)	✗	[.osm.bz2]
Great Britain	[.osm.pbf] (682 MB)	[.shp.zip]	[.osm.bz2]
Greece	[.osm.pbf] (98 MB)	[.shp.zip]	[.osm.bz2]
Hungary	[.osm.pbf] (79 MB)	[.shp.zip]	[.osm.bz2]

6. In the next list, select **England**, you can see your selection on the map located at the right-hand side of the web page, as shown in the following screenshot:

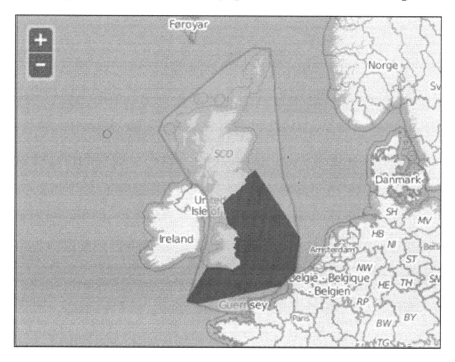

7. Now, you will see a list of all the counties. Select the **.shp.zip** column from the county of **Buckinghamshire**:

Sub Region	Quick Links		
	.osm.pbf	.shp.zip	.osm.bz2
Buckinghamshire	[.osm.pbf] (6.8 MB)	[.shp.zip]	[.osm.bz2]
Cambridgeshire	[.osm.pbf] (13.2 MB)	[.shp.zip]	[.osm.bz2]
Cheshire	[.osm.pbf] (11.6 MB)	[.shp.zip]	[.osm.bz2]
Cornwall	[.osm.pbf] (8.9 MB)	[.shp.zip]	[.osm.bz2]

8. A download will start. When it finishes, you will get a file called `buckinghamshire-latest.shp.zip`. Unzip it.

At this point, we have just obtained the data (several shp files). The next procedure will show us how to convert this file into SQL insertion scripts.

Extracting spatial data from an shp file

In the unzipped folder are shp files; each of them stores a particular feature of the geography of this county. We will focus on the shp named `buildings.shp`.

Now, we will extract this data stored in the shp file. We will convert this data to a sql script so that we can insert its data into the `tbl_buildings` table. For this, we will use a Postgis tool called shp2pgSQL. Perform the following steps for extracting spatial data from an shp file:

1. Open a command window with the cmd command.

2. Go to the unzipped folder.

3. Type the following command:

   ```
   shp2pgsql -g the_geom buildings.shp tbl_buildings > buildings.sql
   ```

4. Open the script with Notepad.

5. Delete the following lines from the script:

   ```
   CREATE TABLE "tbl_buildings"(gid serial, "osm_id" varchar(20),
   "name" varchar(50), "type" varchar(20), "timestamp" varchar (30)
   ); ALTER TABLE "tbl_buildings" ADD PRIMARY KEY (gid);
   SELECT AddGeometryColumn('','tbl_buildings','geom','0','MULTIPOLYG
   ON',2);
   ```

6. Save the script. Open and run it with the pgAdmin query editor.

7. Open the table; you must have at least 13363 new registers. Keep in mind that this number can change when new updates come.

Importing shp files with a graphical tool

There is another way to import an shp file into our table; we could use a graphical tool called postgisgui for this. To use this tool, perform the following steps:

1. In the file explorer, open the folder: `C:\Program Files\PostgreSQL\9.3\bin\postgisgui`.

2. Execute the `shp2pgsql-gui` application. Once this is done, we will see the following window:

3. Configure the connection with the server. Click on the **View Connections Details...** button.

4. Set the data to connect to the server, as shown in the following screenshot:

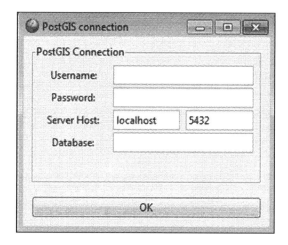

5. Click the **Add File** button. Select the `points.shp` file.

6. Once selected, type the following parameters in the **Import List** section:

   ○ **Mode**: In this field, type `Append`

   ○ **SRID**: In this field, type `4326`

   ○ **Geo column**: In this field, type `the_geom`

   ○ **Table**: In this field, type `tbl_landmarks`

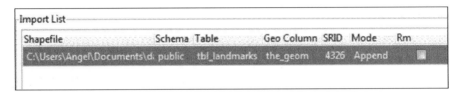

7. Click on the **Import** button. The import process will fail and show you the following message:

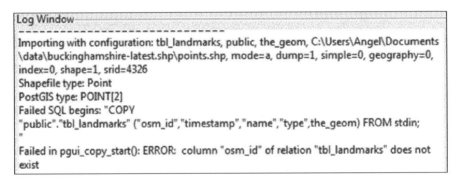

This is because the structure is not the same as shown in the shp and in our table. There is no way to indicate to the tool which field we don't want to import. So, the only way for us to solve this problem is let the tool create a new table and after this, change the structure. This can be done by following these steps:

8. Go to **pgAdmin** and drop the **tbl_landmarks** table. Change the mode to **Create** in the **Import** list. Click on the **Import** button.

9. Now, the import process is successful, but the table structure has changed. Go to the PGAdmin again, refresh the data, and edit the table structure to be the same as it was before:

    ° Change the name of the **geom** field to `the_geom`.

    ° Change the name of the **osm_id** field to `id`.

    ° Drop the **Timestamp** field.

    ° Drop the primary key constraint and add a new one attached to the **id** field. For that, right-click on **Constraints** in the left panel.

    ° Navigate to **New Object | New Primary Key** and type `pk_landmarks_id`. In the **Columns** tab, add the **id** field.

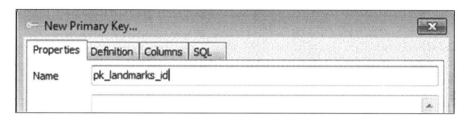

10. Now, we have two spatial tables, one with data that contains positions represented as the PostGIS type, `POINT (tbl_landmarks)`, and the other with polygons, represented by PostGIS with the type, `MULTIPOLYGON(tbl_buildings)`. Now, I would like you to import the data contained in the `roads.shp` file, using one of the two previously viewed methods.

11. The following table has data that represents the path of different highways, streets, roads, and so on, which belong to this area in the form of lines, represented by PostGIS with the `MULTILINESTRING` type. When it's imported, change its name to `tbl_roads` and adjust the columns to the structure used for the other tables in this chapter. Here's an example of how the imported data must look like, as you can see the spatial data is show in its binary form in the following table:

id character var	name character var	type character varying(16)	the_geom geometry(MultiLineString)
2785	Maidenhead	motorway_link	0105000000010000000010200
2786	Huntercombe	motorway_link	0105000000010000000010200
2790	Rectory Roa	residential	0105000000010000000010200
3419	Cedar Chase	residential	0105000000010000000010200
131622	London Orbi	motorway	0105000000010000000010200
131631	London Orbi	motorway	0105000000010000000010200
344157	Western Ave	trunk	0105000000010000000010200
824544	Taplow FP12	footway	0105000000010000000010200

In the next chapter, we will learn how to show this in a way that can be easier to understand for human beings. Excellent! Now that we have learned how to fill our spatial data tables, we are ready to generate selection and filtering queries that will help us to obtain a lot of information that could be very difficult to get (if not impossible) using a different approach. In the coming chapters, we will set up QGIS projects to be able to check what the data looks like and whether the projection of the data is right.

Summary

In this chapter, you learned some basic concepts of GIS (such as WKT, EWKT, and SRS), which are fundamental for working with the GIS data. Now, you are able to craft your own spatial insertion queries or import this data into your own data tables.

In the next chapter, we will see how to exploit this combination of your own as well as external data, using the appropriate SQL spatial extension commands to filter and select data.

There are several ways to create a database or table and you can use the one that fulfills your needs or simply the one that you like the most without any differences in the final result.

In the next chapter, we will learn how to fill these tables by obtaining data from publicly open and freely available sources.

4
Selecting and Filtering GIS Queries

We could say the very existence of PostGIS depends on the ability to develop spatial queries and bring them to the user; therefore, this chapter is important. In the previous chapter, we loaded a lot of data into our data tables; all this spatial data isn't very useful if we don't have the appropriate tools needed to exploit and extract the necessary information from it. This is what spatial queries are about. They provide a way to process thousands or even millions of records in a relatively shorter period of time.

If we understand the way spatial queries work, we could easily develop or adapt existing spatial queries, which will help us to extract the hidden treasure of the valuable that is buried below hundreds of thousands of records stored in our spatial data tables.

We'll learn how to use the set of tools that PostGIS gives us in the form of spatial functions, and to develop amazing spatial queries that will probably put a smile on the faces of our bosses and clients. In this chapter, we will cover the following topics:

- Learning how to obtain useful information from our spatial tables by using nonspatial queries

- Reviewing some of the most useful spatial functions through practical examples

- Learning how to develop queries that can access data from two databases at the same time (nested queries are beyond the scope of this book)

- Developing spatial queries that apply all the knowledge that has been acquired

Grouping data

In the previous chapter, we imported spatial data from several cities in England. This could be very useful in adding fields that would help us to classify and group this data by a region, state, or city. So, let's add a new field called town to the tbl_landmarks table using the following query:

```
ALTER TABLE tbl_landmarks ADD COLUMN town varchar(30);
```

Adapt this query to add the same field to the other tables contained inside the Real_World database. This way, we will have a way to group data and the spatial queries that we develop could be faster, because they will be able to discriminate between a lot of registers without even accessing the spatial field.

In *Chapter 7, Performance Tuning*, we will see the techniques that will help us to accelerate the performance of our spatial queries. The following is the update query that will mostly be applied after importing data from another city into our data table:

```
UPDATE tbl_landmarks
SET town = 'London'
WHERE town IS null
```

As a convention, we will write the first letter of the towns' names in capital. Now, all the registers have the town field set to London; you can apply this query by changing the town value as you import more data into your table.

Nonspatial queries

In the previous section, we have seen how our existing table can be modified in order to add more fields to it, which can make our data even more valuable. Well, we are now ready to develop our first query. We will get the basic information about it first using the standard function of PostgreSQL, then we will be adding complexities to our queries. It's very important to fully understand and dominate the grouping and filtering of SQL before we can apply the spatial functions. For this reason, we must refresh all these skills first. We will see a set of practical exercises that will help us to get basic information about the data stored in our data tables. The data tables in our databases aren't related to each other, so you can work with each one separately.

We will work with the tbl_buildings table first. Let's check how many registers from London we have stored in our table; to do this, we will run the following query:

```
SELECT COUNT(*) FROM tbl_buildings WHERE town='London'
```

We must get a one-row result whose value differs from this depending on whether there have been updates made to the imported data set, as shown in the following table:

Count
223732

Now, you may want to know the data of how many towns you have loaded into your spatial data table. To do this, you should use the following query:

```
SELECT town FROM tbl_buildings
GROUP BY town ORDER BY town
```

You will get a list of all the towns and information on them, which were added to the spatial data table:

Town
Bristol
Buckinghamshire
London

The following exercise will get you a list of the data of all the different kinds of buildings stored in our data table grouped by town:

```
SELECT town, type FROM tbl_buildings
GROUP BY town, type
ORDER BY town, type
```

We will now get the following result:

Town	Type
Buckinghamshire	agricultural
Buckinghamshire	apartments
Buckinghamshire	attraction
Buckinghamshire	bank
Buckinghamshire	barn
Buckinghamshire	Barn
...	...

The dots in the final record indicate that this is just an extract of the information and that this list of records continues in the real query. However, what if we wanted to know how many of them are in each city? We could add the following to our query:

```
SELECT town, type, COUNT(type) FROM tbl_buildings
GROUP BY town, type
ORDER BY town, type;
```

We will get the following table as the output of this query:

Town	Type	Count
Buckinghamshire	agricultural	3
Buckinghamshire	apartments	40
Buckinghamshire	attraction	5
Buckinghamshire	bank	7
Buckinghamshire	barn	18
Buckinghamshire	Barn	1
...	...	...

Here, we can see a problem, specifically with the barn rows. Now, what if you have registers of the same kind in your data but they're written differently? In this case, barn is written with all the letters in lower case and, in some occurrences, with the first letter as a capital. To solve this problem, we could just standardize the data in our table; in this case, we would decide that all the building types must be written in lower case letters, and update all the data that doesn't fit into this new rule. We could make this adjustment with the following query:

```
UPDATE tbl_buildings SET type = LOWER(type);
```

Now, when we rerun the last query, we get the following result in the barn row:

Town	Type	Count
Buckinghamshire	barn	19

However, what if the data doesn't belong to us? We may be in a situation where we probably only have read access to this specific data source, or for some other reason we are unable to modify the data. In such a case, we just have to modify our original query to address this problem:

```
SELECT town, LOWER(type), COUNT(type)
FROM tbl_buildings
GROUP BY town, LOWER(type)
ORDER BY town, LOWER(type);
```

Now, we might only need information on how many universities there are in London. To find out the number, use the following query:

```
SELECT town, type, COUNT(type) FROM tbl_buildings
WHERE town = 'London' AND type = 'university'
GROUP BY town, type
ORDER BY town, type
```

We will get the following result:

Town	Type	Count(type)
London	university	229

Until now, we have only developed regular queries, but the power of PostGIS has not been used here yet. Before we can develop our first spatial query, we must first at least know the most important and useful set of functions that we can use to build our spatial queries. In the next section, we will review and explain them through practical examples using the data stored in our databases.

There are many spatial functions that you could use. We'll now see some of the most important and useful functions through practical examples using the data loaded in the past chapters.

When we have finished, we will need to know how to enable our database to run queries that use data from two different databases; in this specific case, the `Real_Estate` and the `Real_World` databases will be accessed.

Later on in this chapter, we will see how to set up our databases so we can run queries that use data from both databases. These kinds of queries are called cross database queries.

Spatial functions

In this section, we will see a subset of the most useful spatial functions that can be used to extract the information that we need from the databases. These functions will be illustrated through practical examples mentioned earlier. The functions that we will cover are as follows:

- `ST_Distance`
- `ST_DWithin`
- `ST_Length`
- `ST_Intersects`
- `ST_Within`

The ST_Distance functions (geometry, geometry)

It returns the distance between two geometries in projected units, as we saw in *Chapter 3, Inserting GIS Objects*, which mentions the measurement units in which the spatial coordinate is given. As an example, the POINT(-1.344165 51.381320) position is given in degrees; another geographic reference system could use a different unit of measurement, such as meters or feet. If we want to get the measurement in a specific unit of measurement, we will have to make the appropriate conversion on the fly. We will see examples of how this conversion is made and how we could take this into account when we develop our spatial queries.

As an example, let's take the data in the tbl_landmarks data table from the Real-World database. Suppose we want to know the distance between two schools in feet, in this case, the Wendover House School and the Quarrendon School, both located in Buckinghamshire. We will have to use the following query to get this information:

```
SELECT ST_Distance(p1.the_geom, p2.the_geom) as distance
from tbl_landmarks p1, tbl_landmarks p2
where p1.name='Wendover House School' and p2.name = 'Quarrendon
School'
and p1.town='Buckinghamshire'  and p2.town='Buckinghamshire';
```

The preceding query will give us the following result:

Distance
0.108007596490245

If the distance that you have to measure is on a bigger scale, that is, the distance between larger pieces of terrain, such as countries, it will be better if you use a spatial data field called geography. Explaining this data type is beyond the scope of this book, but let me point out that it is more accurate than a geometric field, though its processing is slower.

This measurement here is given in degrees; if we want to get the measurement in feet, we will have to make the followings considerations:

- One degree comprises of 60 nautical miles
- One nautical mile has 6075 feet

Now, taking this into account, we have to modify our query:

```
SELECT ST_Distance(p1.the_geom, p2.the_geom) * 60 * 6075 AS distance
FROM tbl_landmarks p1, tbl_landmarks p2
WHERE p1.name='Wendover House School' AND p2.name = 'Quarrendon
School'
AND p1.town='Buckinghamshire'  AND p2.town='Buckinghamshire';
```

Following is the result in feet:

Distance
39368.7689206943

The next image shows you the distance graphically; this image was taken from **OpenStreetMap**. As you can see, the distance is the length of a straight line between the two locations:

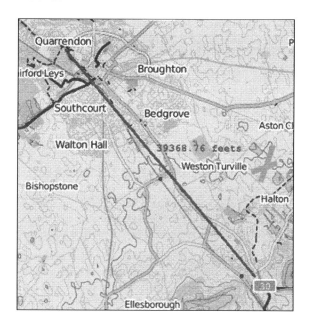

The ST_DWithin function (geometry, geometry, float)

The ST_DWithin function tells us whether the geometry is at a specific distance to another. This distance must be given in the same measurement units that the geographic system uses. Due to the nature of the geometry, it's more of a filtering function that uses indexes, which is very useful to speed up queries, as we will see in *Chapter 7, Performance Tuning*. The following image gives us a graphical example of how this function works:

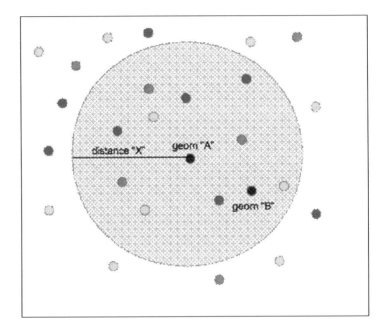

Now, let's perform another exercise. Suppose that we want to know the list of hospitals that are at least a mile from Wendover House School, taking into account that a degree has approximately 69 terrestrial miles (remember that these are shorter than nautical miles). We must develop the query, as follows:

```
SELECT  h.name AS hospital, ST_Distance(s.the_geom, h.the_geom) *69 AS
distance
FROM tbl_landmarks AS h INNER JOIN tbl_landmarks AS s
ON(ST_DWithin(s.the_geom, h.the_geom, (1.00/69)))
WHERE h.type ='hospital'
AND s.name ='Quarrendon School';
```

This leads us to the following result:

Hospital	Distance
Royal Buckinghamshire Hospital	0.572970551308805

As we can see in the following image, the distance between the hospital and the school is less than a mile:

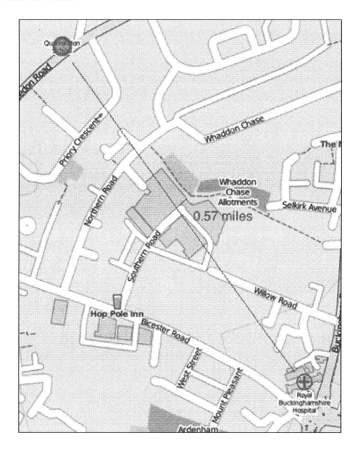

The ST_Length function

The ST_Length function returns the length of a geometrical object if it's a line; the measurement is in the units of its spatial reference. In order to explain this function, we can take an example to find out the length in miles of the primary street called Chapel Street, in Buckinghamshire:

```
SELECT  name, (ST_Length(the_geom))*69 AS length FROM tbl_roads
WHERE name = 'Chapel Street' AND type ='primary' AND town =
'Buckinghamshire';
```

We will get the following result in miles:

name	length
Chapel Street	0.219139309313286

The length of Chapel Street is 0.22 terrestrial miles, also known as statute miles or land miles. Since a mile is equivalent to 1,760 yards, we could say the street is 385.7 yards in length. Most of the streets in our database are divided into segments with the same name. To get the real value of an entire street with this situation, we would have to get the sum of the length of all the segments in the same city, in this manner:

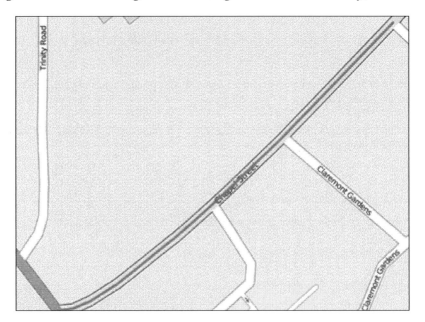

The ST_Intersects function (geometry, geometry)

The ST_Intersects function returns true if the two geometries share any portion of space, in other words, if the two geometries touch or overlap each other:

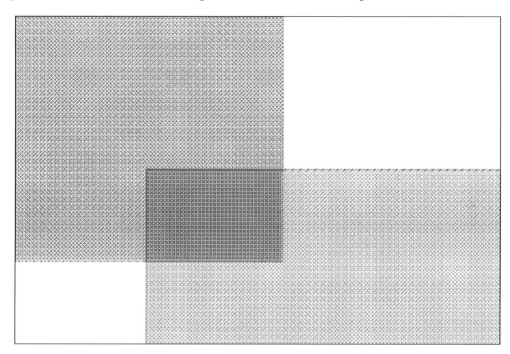

As an example, we would need to get the names of the streets that intersect the Theydon Avenue street in Buckinghamshire:

```
SELECT ri.name FROM tbl_roads AS rk
INNER JOIN tbl_roads AS ri
ON(  st_intersects(rk.the_geom, ri.the_geom) )
WHERE rk.name = 'Theydon Avenue' AND ri.town = 'Buckinghamshire';
```

Here, we are comparing the table with itself; the INNER JOIN filters all the data that doesn't fit in the st_intersects criteria, so the WHERE filter will process much less data.

This query returns the following result; as you can see, it includes itself:

Name
Theydon Avenue
Elm Grove
Elm Grove
Wood Street
Lime Grove
Station Road

In this image, we can see that all these streets intersect each other at some point:

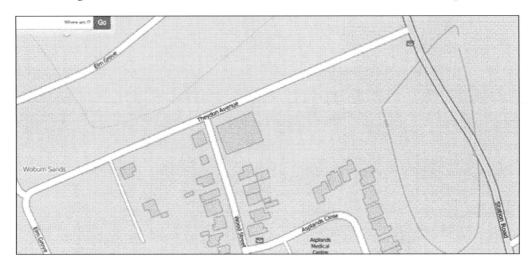

The ST_Within function (geometry A, geometry B)

The ST_Within spatial function simply returns true when Geometry A is completely inside B. Following image explains the concept:

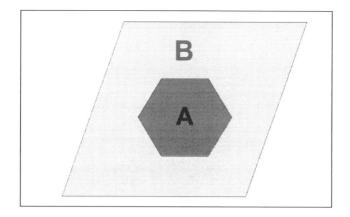

Now, we'll take an example: we may want to know the landmarks present within a specific area. To find out this information, we will set this area using the ST_ GeomFromText function:

```
SELECT name, type FROM tbl_landmarks
WHERE  ST_Within(the_geom, ST_GeomFromText('Polygon(( -0.988 51.999,
-0.971 52.003, -0.9665 51.9913, -0.9805 51.9895, -0.988 51.999 ))',
4326))
ORDER BY name, type;
```

We will get a result that shows us 21 rows:

Name	Type
Buckingham School	School
	Convenience
	Convenience
	Fuel
	mini_roundabout
...	...

OpenStreetMaps doesn't allow us to draw directly on the web page, so to show this polygon graphically, I have chosen to use QGIS:

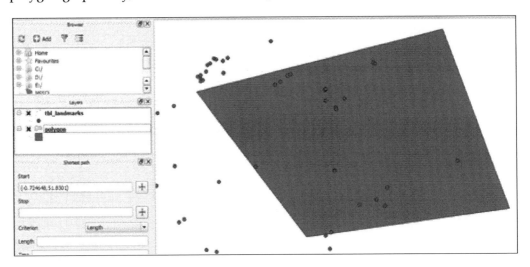

In the next chapter, I will show you how to graphically present the data stored in the tables and queries that we have developed.

Queries that use data from two databases

Now that we have applied some of the most frequently used spatial functions, we could use them to ask our databases some useful information that could be of interest to the company's management or even possible clients.

However, before we start, we have to realize that we have two separate databases and PostgresSQL doesn't support, at least not natively, queries to multiple databases. How can we build a query that uses data from both databases at the same time? The answer lies in installing the Postgres_FWD extension.

The Postgres_FWD module

The `Postgres_FWD` module serves as an extension for PostgreSQL, as PostGIS allows access to data stored in databases that are different from the one in use; you can even access data from remote servers. This module allows us to create a foreign data wrapper, which can be used as a local data table.

The following are the instructions you can use to install and configure it for our databases (in *Chapter 7, Performance Tuning,* you can see how to speed up the performance of each database):

1. Access the `Real-Estate` database using PGAdmin.

2. Open a SQL command window.

3. Execute the following command to create the extension:

    ```
    CREATE EXTENSION postgres_fdw;
    ```

4. Then, execute this command to create the remote server; in this case, it is the same as the local, so we will call the remote server `real_world_server`:

    ```
    CREATE SERVER real_world_server  FOREIGN DATA WRAPPER postgres_fdw
    OPTIONS (host 'localhost', dbname 'Real-World');
    ```

5. Then, we have to map the user who will execute the queries in the remote server:

    ```
    CREATE USER MAPPING FOR CURRENT_USER SERVER   real_world_server
    OPTIONS (user 'postgres', password '123456');
    ```

6. Lastly, we must create a remote table to access these tables as if they were local; in this case, we have named the remote and local tables differently to avoid confusion; the landmarks table would be the link to the `tbl_landmarks` remote table:

    ```
    CREATE FOREIGN TABLE landmarks (id character varying(11),   name
    character varying(48),   type character varying(16),   the_geom
    geometry(Point,4326),   town character(30))  SERVER real_world_
    server OPTIONS (table_name 'tbl_landmarks');
    ```

Downloading the example code

You can download the example code files from your account at `http://www.packtpub.com` for all the Packt Publishing books you have purchased. If you purchased this book elsewhere, you can visit `http://www.packtpub.com/support` and register to have the files e-mailed directly to you.

We must repeat step 6 to add all the other spatial tables to the real estate database. The following figure represents how the databases must be configured:

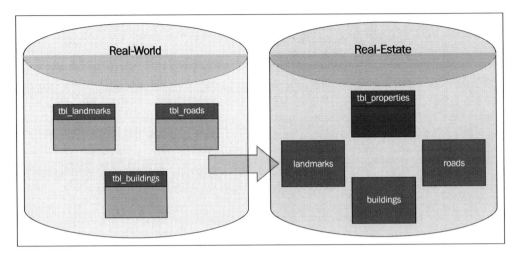

As you can see there is a link between the tables of the **Real-World** database and the **Real-Estate** database, so now it's possible to throw queries as if they were local tables.

Developing spatial queries with our own data

Finally, we can develop the desired spatial queries with our own data. In this section, we will solve a series of possible information requests using the spatial function that was shown to you in the previous section. It's very important to have the basic concepts clear, in order to develop or adapt these queries to our own problem.

We will start with a question that was asked in the first chapter: which houses are located at least 10 miles away from the local supermarket of a specific town? In this case, we will take the city of London as an example; let's get a list of supermarkets in London:

```
SELECT id, name, type FROM landmarks
WHERE type = 'supermarket' AND town = 'London'
ORDER BY name
```

We will get a list of 540 rows; let's choose one to develop the query:

ID	Name	Type
304690529	£-stretcher	supermarket
1579157125	99p Store	supermarket
3098842500	ADM Food and Wine	supermarket
448750327	Aldi	supermarket
1964335366	Aldi	supermarket
…	…	…

I will choose the `99p` Store supermarket, though not for any particular reason. This row has the `1579157125` ID. To see whether any of our properties is at least 10 miles away from the supermarket, for this query, we must choose the `ST_Dwithin` function. We will query the `tbl_properties` table, looking for houses that fit the filter:

```
SELECT p.id, p.town, p.postal_code, p.street, p.number, ST_Distance(p.
the_geom, l.the_geom)*69.00 AS distance  FROM tbl_properties AS
p INNER JOIN landmarks AS l ON  (l.id = '1579157125' ) WHERE ST_
DWithin(p.the_geom, l.the_geom, 10.00 /69.00)
```

In this case, we can see that our property in London is 9.8 miles away:

ID	Town	Postal_code	Street	Number	Distance
1	London	N7 6PA	Holloway Road	32	9.79768721275219

Now, what if a client is interested in this particular property and asks you about the three closest schools in the area? First, we could develop a query that tells us the distance between the homes in question and all the schools in town:

```
SELECT s.id, s.name, ST_Distance(s.the_geom, p.the_geom)*69.00 AS
distance  FROM landmarks AS s  INNER JOIN tbl_properties AS p  ON
(p.id=1) WHERE s.town ='London' AND s.type = 'school'
```

We get the following list:

ID	Name	Distance
196438	St Andrew's Church of England Primary School	3.97779792566405
228047	St Mary's CE Primary School	6.80375648575588
20694281	Sedgehill School	11.2730843255474
20694282	Torridon Road Junior School	11.3893360006287
…	…	…

We have to organize this list in ascending order and only take the first three records from it:

```
SELECT s.id, s.name, ST_Distance(s.the_geom, p.the_geom)*69.00 AS
distance  FROM landmarks AS s  INNER JOIN tbl_properties AS p  ON
(p.id=1) WHERE s.town ='London' AND s.type = 'school' ORDER BY
distance ASC LIMIT 3
```

Now, we get the following result:

ID	Name	Distance
1862259416		1.02901277371039
389899550	Yerbury Primary School	1.04250291491521
2282281919	Ashmount Primary School	1.32943502876518

In this case, the data doesn't have the name of the closest school, but if the client wants, we can give them the geographic position of it:

```
SELECT s.id, s.name, ST_Distance(s.the_geom, p.the_geom)*69.00 AS
distance, ST_AsEWKT(p.the_geom) AS position  FROM landmarks AS s
INNER JOIN tbl_properties AS p  ON (p.id=1) WHERE s.town ='London' AND
s.type = 'school' ORDER BY distance ASC LIMIT 1
```

We get the following result:

ID	Name	Distance	Position
1862259416		1.02901277371039	SRID=4326;POINT(-0.11619 51.556173)

It is always a good idea to use table views in order to exploit your data and make it more intelligent. You may have sensible data stored in some fields of your data tables and you might want it to be available only to certain users and not to others (as an example, there may be a situation where the final prices of some properties must not be available to the final clients, but only to the sales employees), so the use of table views is always a good option for you to consider.

Summary

In this chapter, you learned how to extract valuable information, using both spatial, nonspatial, and a combination of both these approaches. Two different databases were used here, because one of the book's objectives was to show how to do cross queries. However, it's always preferable to use a single database to store all the information that you need to use, so if you have control over the design of your database system, it's better to use a single one. We covered some of the most useful and generally used spatial functions. We worked with both databases at the same time, exploiting their combined data by using the `Postgres_FWD` extension. In order to see the result of the queries graphically, we directly used a website called OpenStreetMaps. In the next chapter, we will learn how to use the powerful QGIS tool to represent GIS operations in a graphical way.

5
Displaying GIS Data Graphically

In this chapter, we will learn how to graphically see the data stored in our spatial databases. To achieve this goal, we will use a powerful tool called QGIS. We have used this tool in the previous chapter, but we will now take a closer look at it. This chapter isn't a complete and exhaustive guide of QGIS; its objective is to be a practical and useful reference that can achieve this book's goals.

In this chapter, we will cover the following topics:

- Learning the basics of how to use QGIS
- Seeing the data stored in our databases
- Using some additional data formats, besides the data stored in our databases
- Building and using spatial queries from the QGIS interface

Introducing QGIS

QGIS is a powerful, open, and free tool that helps us manage several kinds of spatial data sources, which we can use to combine, transform, or analyze this spatial data. Among these data sources, we can find:

- Vectorial data
- Raster files
- **Web Map Services (WMS)**
- Spatial Databases (PostGIS)

As we have established earlier, this chapter's objective isn't to be a comprehensive guide of QGIS, but an attempt to give the reader a quick walkthrough of some of the most useful features that will be needed in order to exploit data. We will just focus on the functions that will allow us to complete our exercises and fully achieve the objectives of this chapter.

Every time you run QGIS, you start a sort of working session, where you can use your data as you need it. You have a blank space area where you can see the data that you load from several possible data sources and the data types that QGIS supports.

The QGIS application

First, let me show you the main window of QGIS:

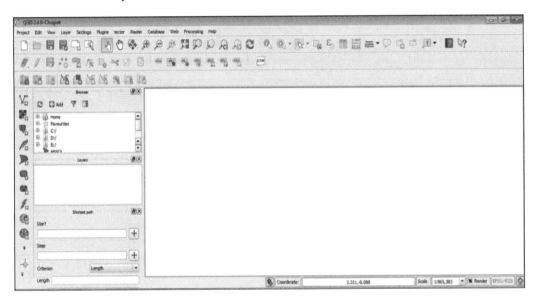

At first glance, it would seem that this software is very complex to use because there are a lot of options, but when you get used to it, you will realize that it is actually very friendly and easy to use. Let's take a look at some of the most important features of this tool:

First, we have the main menu; it shows all the possible actions that we could take with this tool, and we will explain the most important options that we can use later on in this chapter.

In the left-hand section, we have several image icons, and each one represents a data source that QGIS can use. Every time you load data from any source, QGIS adds it to the working session as a layer. You can work with several layers at the same time; we will see this concept in more detail later on in this chapter. Some of the data sources that you can access are as shown in the following table:

Icon	Name	Function
	Add vector layer	You can open vectorial files formats, such as SHP, KML, and so on
	Add raster layer	You can open an image (raster) file as a Geotiff or as a JPG (even if they are not georeferenced)
	Add PostGIS layer	You can access data stored in a PostGIS database by developing a spatial query
	Add WMS/WTMS layer	You can access Web Map Services (WMS) data sources available from your location (via the Internet or Intranet)

Every time you add a layer to your project, you can see it in the blank area on the right-hand side. Since this is the working area, you will see the data you have loaded as one layer above all the previously loaded data. Actually, this is similar to the layers of an onion skin. Here is a look at this working area:

In the bottom section of this area, you can see the geographical position of the mouse cursor when it moves through the working area.

Now, we will see a set of graphical tools that will allow us to move the point of view that a user has of the map; these tools will help him or her focus only on the subarea of his or her interest. Take a look at the following table:

Icon	Name	Function
	Pan Map	You can move the view of the map to any side you want
	Zoom In	You can get a closer look at the image, that is, in the middle point of the working area
	Zoom Out	You can get far away from the middle point of the working area in order to see more of the complete image
	Zoom to native pixel resolution	You can see your data just like it was before when it was originally loaded
	Zoom Full	You can see your data with an optimal zoom that allows the data to fit into the whole blank area

Hands-on with QGIS

Now that we know the basis of QGIS, we can start to use it to see the data that is stored in our data tables. First, we will take a look inside the `tbl_landmarks` table; to do this, we will have to perform the following steps:

1. In the **Layers** menu, select **Add PostGIS Layers**:

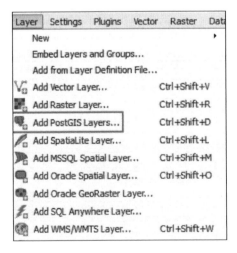

2. Now, you can see a window where you will have to specify the necessary data in order to establish a connection with your PostGIS server:

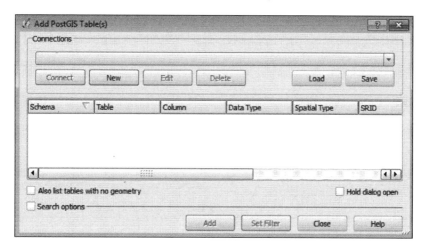

3. Click on the **New** button to create a new connection, and you will see the following window:

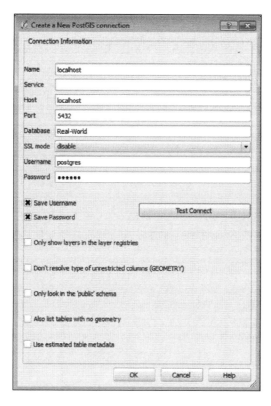

4. Fill it with the appropriate data; you can click on the **Test Connect** button to check that the data is okay. If you are working from your personal machine or think it's secure enough to save your username and password on it, you can check those checkboxes to avoid QGIS from asking you for them every time you connect to the server. Click on the **OK** button to finish.

5. You will see a warning dialog box if you choose to store the username and password; click on **OK** to continue.

6. Now, you are again in the first window; click on the **Connect** button to access your database:

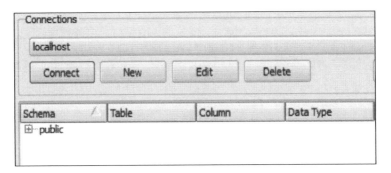

7. You can see that the public schema of your database was added; now click on the + symbol to expand the node:

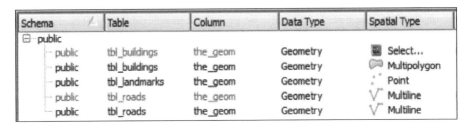

8. We can now see a list of the spatial tables stored in this database; now, we will select the **tbl_landmarks** table and see the following result:

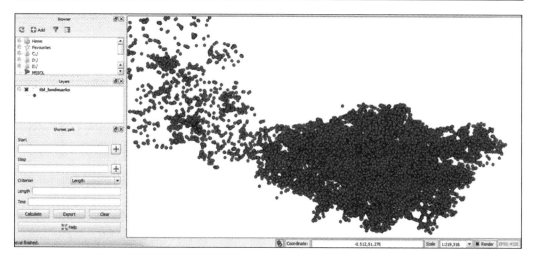

9. We can see a set of all the landmarks that we have stored. On the left-hand side of the window, you can see a section titled Layers. In this section, we can click on the checkbox on the left to see whether the content of this layer is on our map.

There is a problem here. You can see the data, but there isn't any reference of where the landmark is in the context of a city or country. Now, in order to address this problem, we must get the spatial data that gives us the needed contextual reference.

There are a lot of websites that offer commercial and noncommercial data; most of this data is available in public sources, such as the web pages of government agencies. In this case, we will use a freely available shp file with the boundaries of the United Kingdom, which you will find from the Global Administrative Areas project. You can visit their website at `http://www.gadm.org/country`.

Perform the following steps:

1. Copy the file into the folder of your preference and then click on **Add Vector Layer** in the **Layer** menu:

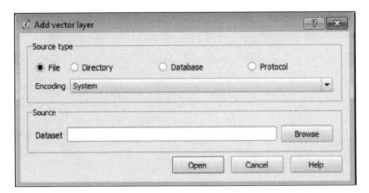

2. When this window shows up on the screen, you must click on the **Browse** button and select the shp file; you will see a window where you will choose **Coordinate Reference System** of your file. In this case, we will choose **WGS 84** and click on the **OK** button, as shown in this screenshot:

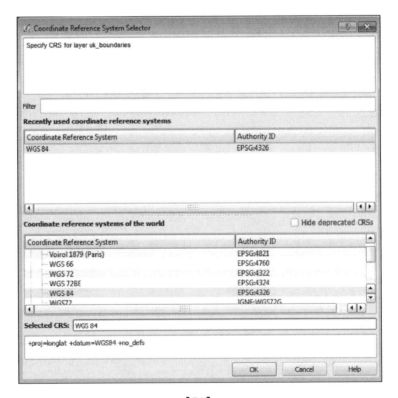

3. After this, we can see the United Kingdom map on the right-hand side.

4. If you load data that uses a different CRS, you can check the on-the-fly transformation option of QGIS by navigating to **Project Properties | CRS | Enable 'on the fly' CRS transformation**. This way all the data will be displayed on the same projection:

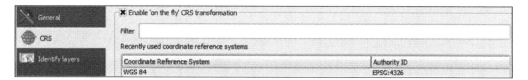

And this is how it must look like:

5. However, now we can't see the landmarks. This is because the landmarks layer is below the boundaries layer; we must correct this by placing the landmarks layer above the boundaries layer. To do this, you must click on the landmarks layer and drag it up:

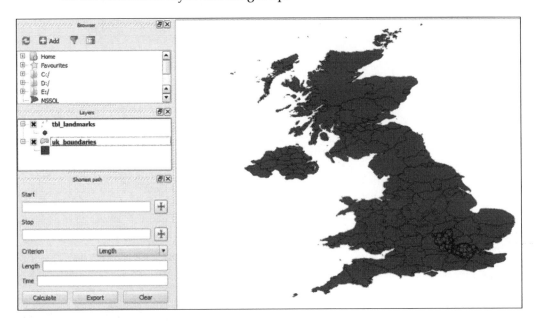

6. Now, we can see both datasets; let's zoom into the area of our interest. To do this, select the **Zoom In** tool and later click on the upper-left corner of the area we want to zoom. Then, drag the mouse cursor to form a square; lastly, drop the mouse button, and you will now see only the area of interest. Repeat these steps until you can see the desired area at the appropriate zoom level:

7. It looks okay now, but maybe it would look better if we change the blue used for the background to white; to do this, we will have to right-click on the layers of the boundaries, and then we will see the following pop-up menu:

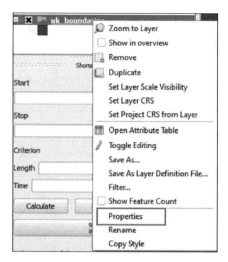

8. Now, we must click on the **Properties** option to access the **Layer Properties** window, so as to be able to change them:

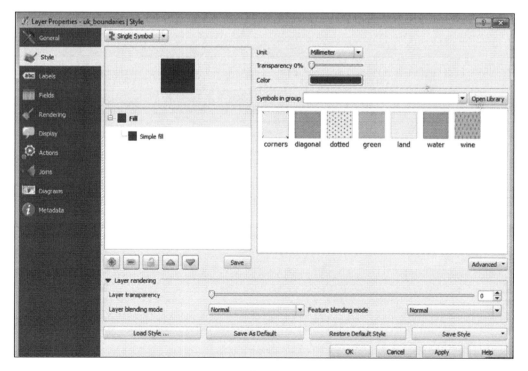

9. We should change the color from blue to white in the color section:

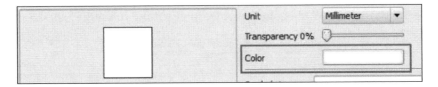

10. Then, click on the **OK** button in the bottom section of the window and we will see a change in the map, as shown in the following screenshot:

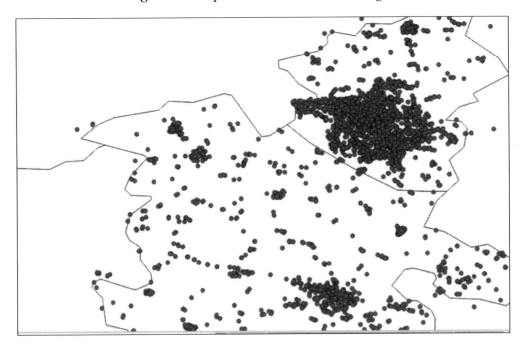

11. It looks a lot better now, so we could help the user even more if we could show a label above the landmark with it's name. To do this, we have to select the properties window of the landmarks layer and then select the **Labels** section on the left-hand side of the window:

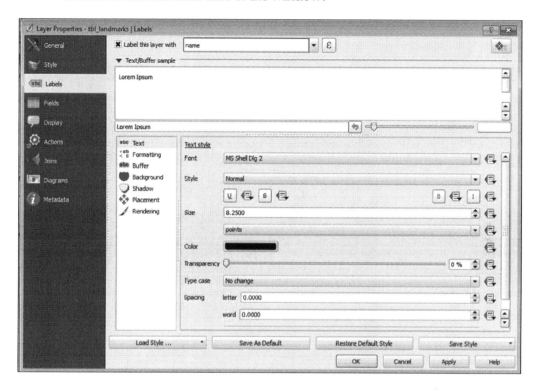

12. We have to click the **Label this layer with checkbox** and select the name field from the list of available data fields on the right-hand side, and then click on the **OK** button, the result will be similar to the following screenshot:

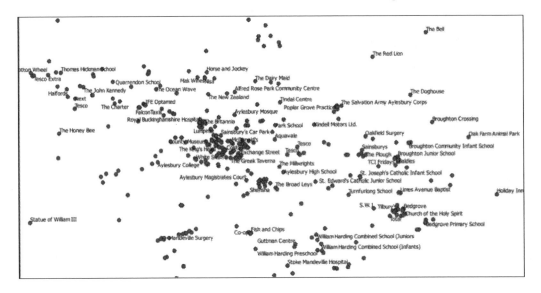

Now, all the labels are shown for all the records with a nonempty name field value.

Don't you think that instead of the white background used here, it would be more useful and interesting to have the image of a terrain? If you agree with me, we will need to get this image from a public data source. Several governmental agencies around the world provide public geographic data of their respective countries. In this case, we will get an image from the national mapping agency of Great Britain, known as "Ordinance Survey". You can get a lot of free spatial data under an open data license. We can find it at Ordnance Survey; you can visit its website at `https://www.ordnancesurvey.co.uk/opendatadownload/products.html` and the license is available at `http://www.ordnancesurvey.co.uk/docs/licences/os-opendata-licence.pdf`. This license allows us to:

- Copy, publish, distribute, and transmit information
- Adapt information
- Exploit information commercially and noncommercially, for example, by combining it with other information
- Include this information in your own product or application

For the following exercise, you must choose to download the GB Overview Maps images. When you download the images, you get two `geotiff` files, `GBOverview.tif` and `GBOverviewPlus.tif`; we will work with the second one. Perform the following steps:

1. First, we must navigate to the **Layers | Add Raster Image** in the main menu.
2. Select the raster file from the folder where it's stored. Now, you will see a screen similar to the following screenshot:

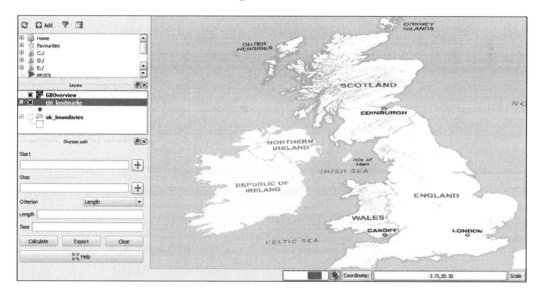

3. You can see a beautiful map, but the data loaded from the database is not visible; you should put the landmark layer above the GBOverview layer, and the result will be similar to that shown in the following screenshot:

4. You can now see the landmarks, but there is a problem; if you want to see the boundaries layer, it doesn't let you view the image layer. In order to correct this situation, we must convert the white color of the boundaries layer to transparent. To do this, first right-click on the boundaries layer and navigate to **Properties | Style** and change fill style to **No Brush**. Then, click on **OK** for the changes to take effect:

5. Put the boundaries layer above the GBOverview layer and you will be able to see the boundaries, as shown in this screenshot:

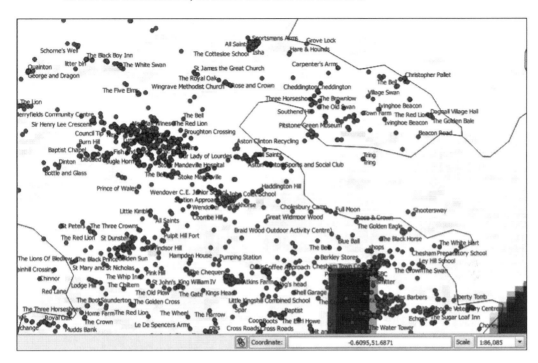

Now, the map looks great, but there is a problem; the landmark data table has a lot of registers, and maybe we only wanted to see data from one specific city or area. We can do this by accessing data from a spatial query, instead of the data table. We will now see how to throw a spatial query from QGIS and display the result set:

6. First, we will remove the landmarks layer. Right-click on the layer and select the option, **remove**; you will see a confirmation dialog. Click on the **OK** button for the change to take effect, and the effects are shown in the following screenshot:

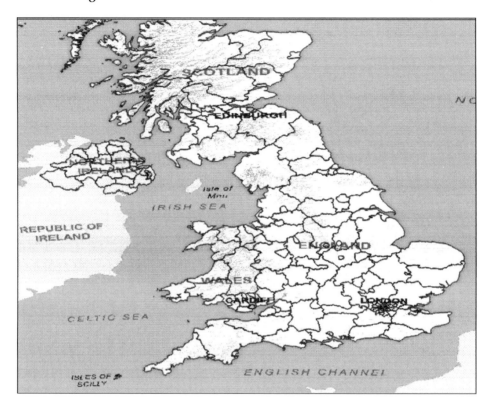

7. Now, you have a map to look at, as the one shown in the previous screenshot. The next step is to develop the spatial query.

We have learned how to load and combine information contained in several types of file formats. We will now see how to add to this combination data directly obtained from spatial queries to our database.

Developing a spatial query from QGIS

It's possible to generate spatial queries from QGIS. Perform the following steps:

1. To do this, navigate to **Layers | PostGIS Layers**. We have to first select **DB Manager** from the database menu option:

2. Once you have selected the option, you will see the **DB Manager** window. There, you must select the **PostGIS** option:

3. Expand the child nodes until you get to the spatial tables stored in the database, and then click on the **SQL window** button. You will see **SQL window**. There, you can write an SQL query as if you were in the PostgreSQL GUI:

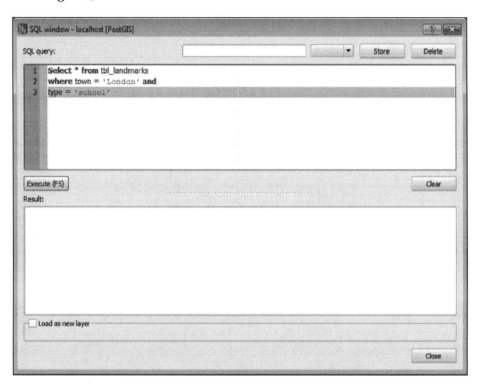

4. Once you have finished, click on the **Execute (F5)** button. If the query is valid, you will get the result set in the **Result** section, as shown in the following screenshot:

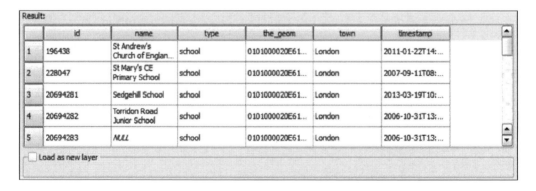

5. To see the graphical representation of the data, we must click on the **Load as a new layer** checkbox. Then, you can specify which fields correspond to the ID and the geometric fields in your database; the ID column should be an integer with a unique value. For this, we have created an additional field called `num` with `serial` as the data type:

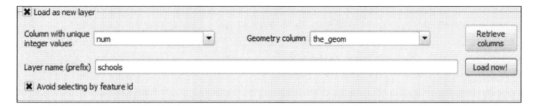

6. You must specify a layer name too. When you are done, you can click on the **Load now!** button to see the new layer:

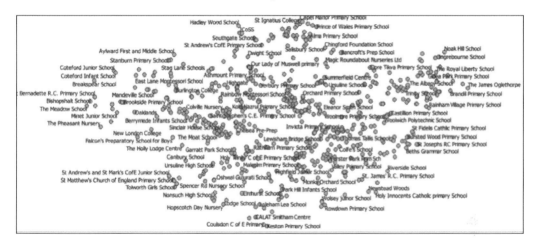

If you put a label related to the **name** field, you can see all the schools in London. You will now be able to repeat the exercises of the previous chapter using this tool. You will see a graphical representation of the data, which when combined with another visual support data, can give to the regular user a much better understanding of the results rather than just seeing it in text form.

Summary

In this chapter, we have learned how to graphically display data stored in both spatial data tables, and raster and vectorial files. By combining them, we can get useful information that our clients and bosses can easily understand and use, even if they don't have any knowledge or training in GIS applications.

In this chapter, we worked with vectorial files similar to the ones in *Chapter 2, Creating Your First GIS Database*. We learned how to save shp data in our spatial data tables, but is this the only kind of file that we can use? What if we get information in a different data format, such as KML? Also, what happened to the raster files? Where can they be stored? In the next chapter, we will answer this and several other questions, by using several kinds of vectorial and raster files.

6
Management of Vectorial and Raster Data with PostGIS

In *Chapter 3*, *Inserting GIS Objects*, we learned how to work with Shapefiles, generating SQL insertion sentences to create and insert appropriate records in our spatial data tables. Shapefiles are some of the most common and useful vectorial files used across the world, but they aren't the only spatial data format available. There are a lot of popular formats out there, and now we will learn how to deal with them. In this chapter, we will see how to transform a file in almost any spatial format to shp.

It seems that the vectorial data is covered now, but what has happened to the raster data? Could it be stored in the spatial database too? Well, the answer is *yes*. In this chapter, we will work with raster data formats. We will insert and retrieve this data into our spatial tables.

To achieve these goals, we will need a special tool that is actually a part of PostGIS's infrastructure; this is a library called **Geospatial Data Abstraction Library (GDAL)**. GDAL allows us to convert spatial data from one format to another. In this chapter, we will see the basics of this powerful tool and how we can interact with it to achieve our goals. In this chapter, we will cover the following topics:

- Learning how to convert almost any kind of vectorial data file into an shp file
- Learning how to use GDAL to transform and re-project raster data files
- Learn how to store and retrieve raster data into our tables

The GDAL/OGR library

Before we can move on with this chapter, we will need to explain what the GDAL/OGR library is, and why it is necessary for us. Well, first let me tell you that GDAL is a translator library used for raster and vector geospatial data formats, and is released under an X/MIT style Open Source License by the **Open Source Geospatial Foundation**. You can visit its official web page at http://www.gdal.org/.

You can use GDAL both as a set of command line utilities, or even as a set of API libraries to add spatial functionality to your applications. This library divides itself in two. Traditionally, the term GDAL is used to design the raster part of the library, and OGR is used for the vector part. Basically, we will use it to transform data from one type to another; in this particular case, we will learn how to transform KML files to shps. Now that we know what GDAL is, it's time to install it into our machine. To do this, you can perform the following steps:

1. Open your favorite web browser and go to GDAL's main page at http://www.gdal.org/.

2. Click on the **Downloads** section, as shown in the following screenshot:

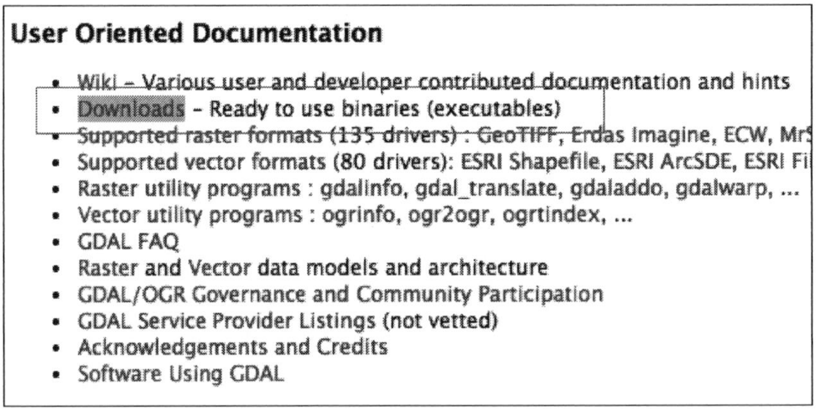

3. In the **GDAL/OGR Binaries** page, go to the **Windows** section and select the first location, as shown in the following screenshot:

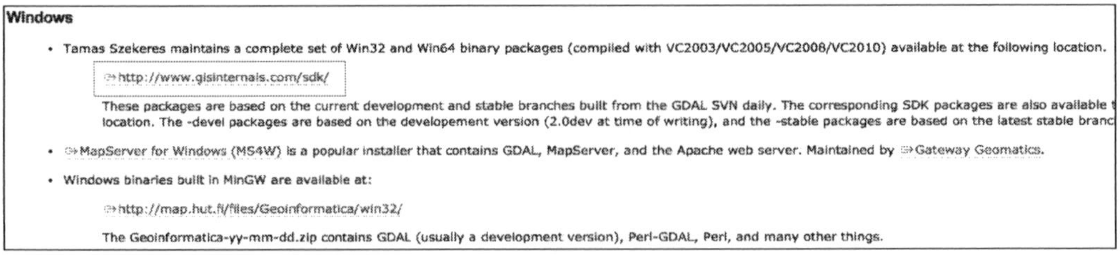

4. Then, you will be redirected to the GIS internals support site; once you're there, select the **Stable Releases** link, as shown in the following screenshot:

The buildsystem provides the following resources to download:

- *Stable Releases* - Packages based on the current (official) MapServer and GDAL releases
- *Stable Branches* - Packages compiled daily based on the MapServer Git and GDAL SVN latest stable branches
- *Development Versions* - Packages compiled daily based on the MapServer Git (master) and GDAL SVN (trunk)
- *Development Kits* - Support files to compile mapserver and gdal by yourself
- *Archive Versions* - Older MapServer/GDAL releases, based on previous compilations (not compiled regularly)
- *MapServer MapManager* - MapServer MapManager desktop application to configure map files

5. Here, you will see a table with different versions of GDAL; for our purposes, we will choose the last one, as shown in the following screenshot:

Stable Releases

The following packages are compiled based on packages based on the latest official releases of MapServer and GDAL. It is recommended to use these packages testing and in production environments.

Compiler	Platform	Downloads	Package Information
MSVC 2005	win32	*release-1400-gdal-1-11-1-mapserver-6-4-1*	*information*
MSVC 2005	x64	*release-1400-x64-gdal-1-11-1-mapserver-6-4-1*	*information*
MSVC 2008	win32	*release-1500-gdal-1-11-1-mapserver-6-4-1*	*information*
MSVC 2008	x64	*release-1500-x64-gdal-1-11-1-mapserver-6-4-1*	*information*
MSVC 2010	win32	*release-1600-gdal-1-11-1-mapserver-6-4-1*	*information*
MSVC 2010	x64	*release-1600-x64-gdal-1-11-1-mapserver-6-4-1*	*information*

6. Then, we will have to choose which component we want to install in our computer; you must choose **gdal-111-1600-x64-core.msi**:

File name	File date	Size	Description
GDAL-1.11.1.win-amd64-py2.7.msi	2014-12-14 21:17:00	496 kB	Installer for the GDAL python bindings (requires to install the GDAL core)
mapserver-6.4.1-1600-x64-core.msi	2014-12-14 21:17:22	23421 kB	MapServer installer with IIS registration support
gdal-111-1600-x64-oracle.msi	2014-12-14 21:17:13	957 kB	Installer for the GDAL Oracle plugin (must be installed to the same directory as the GDAL core)
GDAL-1.11.1.win-amd64-py3.3.msi	2014-12-14 21:17:01	464 kB	Installer for the GDAL python bindings (requires to install the GDAL core)
GDAL-1.11.1.win-amd64-py3.1.msi	2014-12-14 21:17:01	512 kB	Installer for the GDAL python bindings (requires to install the GDAL core)
GDAL-1.11.1.win-amd64-py3.2.msi	2014-12-14 21:17:01	512 kB	Installer for the GDAL python bindings (requires to install the GDAL core)
gdal-111-1600-x64-ecw.msi	2014-12-14 21:17:10	3584 kB	Installer for the GDAL ECW plugin (must be installed to the same directory as the GDAL core)
gdal-111-1600-x64-filegdb.msi	2014-12-14 21:17:11	2122 kB	Installer for the GDAL FileGDB plugin (must be installed to the same directory as the GDAL core)
gdal-111-1600-x64-core.msi	2014-12-14 21:17:09	20830 kB	Generic installer for the GDAL core components
gdal-111-1600-x64-mrsid.msi	2014-12-14 21:17:12	2914 kB	Installer for the GDAL MrSID plugin (must be installed to the same directory as the GDAL core)

7. Once you have selected the link, the download will start. When it is finished, you must install it on your computer.

8. Then, you will see the installation wizard; click on the **Next** button for the installation process to begin, as shown in the following screenshot:

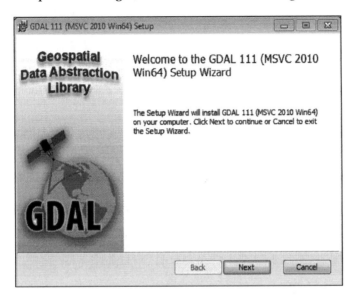

9. Accept the terms of the license and click on the **Next** button.

10. Select the **Typical** option, as shown in the following screenshot:

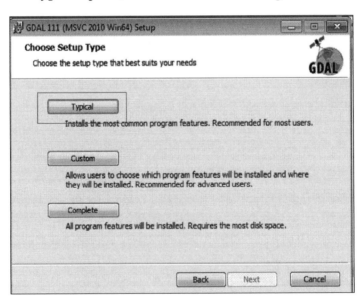

11. Then, click the **Install** button. The application wizard starts to copy the appropriate files and registers the components into your computer.

12. When the wizard finishes installing the application, you will see a screen similar to the following screenshot:

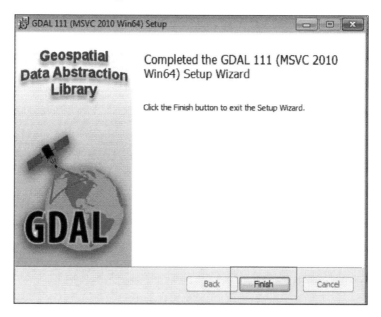

13. Click on the **Finish** button to close this window.

14. If you want the GDAL tools and application to be available from all the locations in a msdos-like command interface, add the following path to the PATH environment, C:\Program Files\GDAL, as we did in *Chapter 2, Creating Your First Spatial Database*.

15. Restart your computer for the changes to take effect.

Working with GDAL/OGR commands

Now that the GDAL library is installed on our computer, let's run some commands to test whether the installation was successful. Open a command line window and write the following commands:

1. First, let's check the library's version:

```
gdalinfo –version
```

We must get the following result:

```
GDAL 1.11.1, released 2014/09/24
```

Now, to see the raster formats that this tool can process, we must run the following command:

```
gdalinfo --formats
```

We will get a list of the available formats that the tool is able to read and sometimes write; the following screenshot is an extract of this list:

```
C:\Users\Angel\Documents>gdalinfo --formats
Supported Formats:
  BAG (ro): Bathymetry Attributed Grid
  FITS (rw+): Flexible Image Transport System
  GMT (rw): GMT NetCDF Grid Format
  HDF4 (ros): Hierarchical Data Format Release 4
  HDF4Image (rw+): HDF4 Dataset
  HDF5 (ros): Hierarchical Data Format Release 5
  HDF5Image (ro): HDF5 Dataset
  netCDF (rw+s): Network Common Data Format
  VRT (rw+v): Virtual Raster
  GTiff (rw+vs): GeoTIFF
  NITF (rw+vs): National Imagery Transmission Format
  RPFTOC (rovs): Raster Product Format TOC format
  ECRGTOC (rovs): ECRG TOC format
  HFA (rw+v): Erdas Imagine Images (.img)
  SAR_CEOS (rov): CEOS SAR Image
  CEOS (rov): CEOS Image
  JAXAPALSAR (rov): JAXA PALSAR Product Reader (Level 1.1/1.5)
  GFF (rov): Ground-based SAR Applications Testbed File Format (.gff)
  ELAS (rw+v): ELAS
  AIG (rov): Arc/Info Binary Grid
  AAIGrid (rwv): Arc/Info ASCII Grid
  GRASSASCIIGrid (rov): GRASS ASCII Grid
  SDTS (rov): SDTS Raster
  DTED (rwv): DTED Elevation Raster
  PNG (rwv): Portable Network Graphics
  JPEG (rwv): JPEG JFIF
  MEM (rw+): In Memory Raster
  JDEM (rov): Japanese DEM (.mem)
  GIF (rwv): Graphics Interchange Format (.gif)
  BIGGIF (rov): Graphics Interchange Format (.gif)
  ESAT (rov): Envisat Image Format
  BSB (rov): Maptech BSB Nautical Charts
  XPM (rwv): X11 PixMap Format
  BMP (rw+v): MS Windows Device Independent Bitmap
  DIMAP (rov): SPOT DIMAP
  AirSAR (ro): AirSAR Polarimetric Image
  RS2 (ros): RadarSat 2 XML Product
  PCIDSK (rw+v): PCIDSK Database File
  PCRaster (rw): PCRaster Raster File
  ILWIS (rw+v): ILWIS Raster Map
  SGI (rw+): SGI Image File Format 1.0
  SRTMHGT (rwv): SRTMHGT File Format
  Leveller (rw+): Leveller heightfield
  Terragen (rw+): Terragen heightfield
  ISIS3 (rov): USGS Astrogeology ISIS cube (Version 3)
  ISIS2 (rw+v): USGS Astrogeology ISIS cube (Version 2)
  PDS (rov): NASA Planetary Data System
  TIL (rov): EarthWatch .TIL
```

GDAL supports 118 different types of raster files.

2. Now, if we want to do the same for vectorial files, we will use the following command:

```
ogrinfo --formats
```

We will get a list of 65 types of files:

```
Supported Formats:
    -> "ESRI Shapefile" (read/write)
    -> "MapInfo File" (read/write)
    -> "UK .NTF" (readonly)
    -> "SDTS" (readonly)
    -> "TIGER" (read/write)
    -> "S57" (read/write)
    -> "DGN" (read/write)
    -> "VRT" (readonly)
    -> "REC" (readonly)
```

. . .

3. Now, let's focus on the vectorial files; our objective is to learn the basics to transform any of these 64 different data types (except shp type, obviously) into an shp file that we can insert directly into our PostGIS spatial data tables. The command that we will use is `ogr2ogr`, and the syntax is:

```
ogr2ogr -f "Format name" output_file input_file
```

4. Let's see how to use this tool through an example that transforms a KML file into an shp file. Let's take an example where we want to include the United Kingdom postal code boundaries in our spatial database, but this time instead of getting this information from an shp file, as we did in *Chapter 3, Inserting GIS Objects*, we get it in a KML file from `http://www.freemaptools.com/`. It comes with a lot of free spatial resources that you could find useful. The file is named `postcodes-boudaries.kml`. Now, we have to convert this KML file into an shp file so that we can insert it into a spatial table. The command to fulfill this objective is:

```
ogr2ogr -f "ESRI Shapefile" postcode-boundaries.shp postcode-boundaries.kml
```

5. We can adapt this example to transform any other supported data; all we need to do is change the name of the input and output files, and OGR will use the right transformation to obtain an shp file. If OGR doesn't know how to handle a particular format or if the file is damaged, we will get an error message telling us the list of drivers that OGR tried to use.

Working with raster files

Raster files represent a terrain by its image at a certain altitude and contain metadata that allows setting the image in the right place above an electronic map. Working with raster data is a little different from working with vectorial data. First, we must define a table with a field of raster type instead of the geometric type that we have used in previous chapters.

We will need to use the GDAL `raster2pgsql` command; this tool will generate the appropriate SQL sentences to create the spatial table and insert data into it. We will work with the `GBOverview.tif` file that we used in *Chapter 5, Displaying GIS Data Graphically*.

Before we start, we need to get a little information on this file; in this case, we must know what projection it is using. To get this information, we must use a GDAL command tool called `gdalinfo`. This tool gives us a lot of useful information on a specific raster file. Now, we will use the following command:

```
gdalinfo GBOverview.tif
```

When we run it, we will get the following output:

```
Driver: GTiff/GeoTIFF
Files: GBOverview.tif
Size is 4000, 3200
Coordinate System is:
PROJCS["OSGB 1936 / British National Grid",
    GEOGCS["OSGB 1936",
        DATUM["OSGB_1936",
            SPHEROID["Airy 1830",6377563.396,299.3249646000044,
                AUTHORITY["EPSG","7001"]],
            AUTHORITY["EPSG","6277"]],
        PRIMEM["Greenwich",0],
        UNIT["degree",0.0174532925199433],
        AUTHORITY["EPSG","4277"]],
    PROJECTION["Transverse_Mercator"],
    PARAMETER["latitude_of_origin",49],
    PARAMETER["central_meridian",-2],
    PARAMETER["scale_factor",0.9996012717],
    PARAMETER["false_easting",400000],
    PARAMETER["false_northing",-100000],
```

```
    UNIT["metre",1,
        AUTHORITY["EPSG","9001"]],
    AUTHORITY["EPSG","27700"]]
Origin = (-649749.999999999880000,1449750.000000000500000)
Pixel Size = (500.000000000000000,-500.000000000000170)
Metadata:
  AREA_OR_POINT=Area
  TIFFTAG_COPYRIGHT=Ordnance Survey. Crown copyright and database right
2013
  TIFFTAG_DATETIME=2013:08:12 13:27:15
  TIFFTAG_RESOLUTIONUNIT=3 (pixels/cm)
  TIFFTAG_SOFTWARE=Adobe Photoshop CS6 (Windows)
  TIFFTAG_XRESOLUTION=10
  TIFFTAG_YRESOLUTION=10
Image Structure Metadata:
  COMPRESSION=LZW
  INTERLEAVE=PIXEL
Corner Coordinates:
Upper Left  ( -649750.000, 1449750.000) ( 21d55'22.41"W, 61d27'54.60"N)
Lower Left  ( -649750.000, -150250.000) ( 16d 0'12.44"W, 47d41'10.18"N)
Upper Right ( 1350250.000, 1449750.000) ( 16d 9' 2.77"E, 61d43'17.34"N)
Lower Right ( 1350250.000, -150250.000) ( 10d42'41.48"E, 47d50'21.53"N)
Center      (  350250.000,  649750.000) (  2d47'32.76"W, 55d44'18.95"N)
Band 1 Block=4000x32 Type=Byte, ColorInterp=Red
Band 2 Block=4000x32 Type=Byte, ColorInterp=Green
Band 3 Block=4000x32 Type=Byte, ColorInterp=Blue
```

This is a lot of information! But, in this case, we just need some data: `AUTHORITY["EPSG","27700"]` is the ID of the projection that was used to create this image, in this case, it is `OSGB 1936 / British National Grid`. As we've said in the past, all the data that we will use must be projected in the EPSG 4326 WGS 84 projection. We must make a re-projection of the data before we can insert it into the database. Now, we must use another GDAL tool called `gdalwrap`. This tool will generate a new `geotif` file with the right projection. The following command is used to run:

```
gdalwrap -s_srs EPSG:27700 -t_srs EPSG:4326 GBOverview.tif
GBOverview4326.tif
```

Here, we tell GDAL that we want to generate a new file that we called
GBOverview4326.tif previously, from the old one with a different SRS, which is, in
this case, WGS 84. If everything goes well, we will get the new file in the same folder.
We can check the properties of the new file:

```
gdalinfo GBOverview4326.tif
```

From this, we will get the following outcome:

```
Driver: GTiff/GeoTIFF
Files: GBOverview4326.tif
Size is 5515, 2207
Coordinate System is:
GEOGCS["WGS 84",
    DATUM["WGS_1984",
        SPHEROID["WGS 84",6378137,298.257223563,
            AUTHORITY["EPSG","7030"]],
        AUTHORITY["EPSG","6326"]],
    PRIMEM["Greenwich",0],
    UNIT["degree",0.0174532925199433],
    AUTHORITY["EPSG","4326"]]
Origin = (-21.921732742690157,62.924895838648141)
Pixel Size = (0.006902997508602,-0.006902997508602)
Metadata:
  AREA_OR_POINT=Area
  TIFFTAG_COPYRIGHT=Ordnance Survey. Crown copyright and database right
2013
  TIFFTAG_DATETIME=2013:08:12 13:27:15
  TIFFTAG_RESOLUTIONUNIT=3 (pixels/cm)
  TIFFTAG_SOFTWARE=Adobe Photoshop CS6 (Windows)
  TIFFTAG_XRESOLUTION=10
  TIFFTAG_YRESOLUTION=10
Image Structure Metadata:
  INTERLEAVE=PIXEL
```

```
Corner Coordinates:
Upper Left  ( -21.9217327,  62.9248958) ( 21d55'18.24"W, 62d55'29.63"N)
Lower Left  ( -21.9217327,  47.6899803) ( 21d55'18.24"W, 47d41'23.93"N)
Upper Right (  16.1482985,  62.9248958) ( 16d 8'53.87"E, 62d55'29.63"N)
Lower Right (  16.1482985,  47.6899803) ( 16d 8'53.87"E, 47d41'23.93"N)
Center      (  -2.8867171,  55.3074381) (  2d53'12.18"W, 55d18'26.78"N)
Band 1 Block=5515x1 Type=Byte, ColorInterp=Red
Band 2 Block=5515x1 Type=Byte, ColorInterp=Green
Band 3 Block=5515x1 Type=Byte, ColorInterp=Blue
```

Now, we can see the new projection of this file in the following part of the outcome:

```
AUTHORITY["EPSG","4326"]
```

Inserting raster data into our database

Since we have got a re-projected file, we can continue to insert it into a spatial table. Let's open a command window and go to the directory where the GBOverview4326. tif file is. Now, let's run the following command:

```
raster2pgsql GBOverviwe.tif –F overview > overview.sql
```

The -F option means that we want to create a field that holds the file name of the raster file. The overview function sets the name of the spatial table, and > overview.sql specifies the name of the file where the SQL script must be saved.

After running this command, we will get a file named overview.sql; if we open it, we will see the following outcome:

```
BEGIN;
CREATE TABLE "overview" ("rid" serial PRIMARY KEY,"rast"
raster,"filename" text);
INSERT INTO "overview" ("rast","filename") VALUES ('01000003
000000000000407F400300000000407FC0FFFFFFFF2BD423C102000000161
F364100000000000000000000000000000000008… 9E9E9E9EA'::raster,
'GBOverview.tif');
END;
```

Obviously, this is a shorter version of the insertion command. This one holds the image data in the first field, and in the second field, the name of the file where the image was extracted is set.

Now, let's run this SQL script. You may have wanted to use the graphical tool to do it, but as the file is very large, the SQL graphical tool has problems loading it. It will be better to do this using the text command, by performing the following steps:

1. Open a command window.
2. Go to the folder where the SQL script is saved.
3. Log in into the `Real-world` database using the following command:

   ```
   psql -U postgres -d Real-World
   ```

4. Run the SQL script with this command:

   ```
   \i overview.sql
   ```

5. If the command is successful, you will see the following echo messages:

   ```
   BEGIN
   CREATE TABLE
   INSERT 0 1
   COMMIT
   ```

Graphically displaying raster data saved in our database

Now that our table is created and filled, you would probably want to check whether the data was correctly loaded. Well, to do this, we will use QGIS again, with the help of the following steps:

1. Open QGIS.
2. Navigate to the **Database | DBManager**.
3. Log in into the `real-world` database.
4. Expand **localhost** and the **public** nodes; once you do this, you will see a screen similar to the following screenshot:

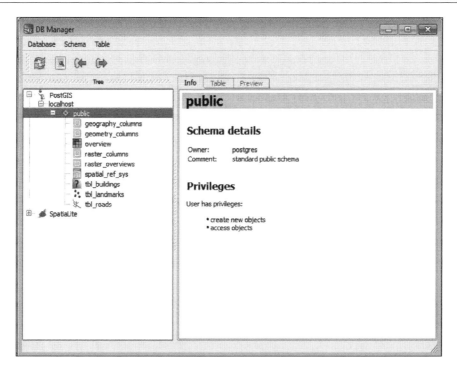

5. Let's select the **overview** table; we will see a sheet with information about the table, as shown in the following screenshot:

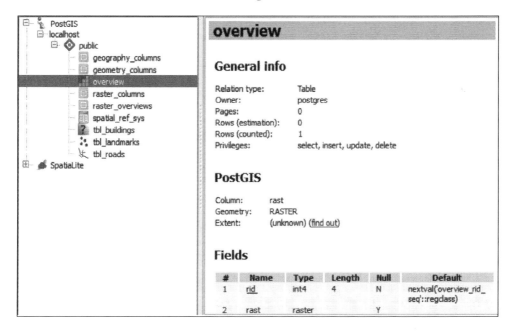

6.   Right-click on the table and select the **Add to canvas** option:

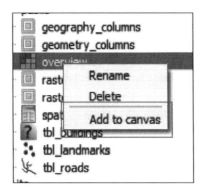

7.   The application starts to load the image onto the canvas. When it finishes, you will see something similar to the following screenshot:

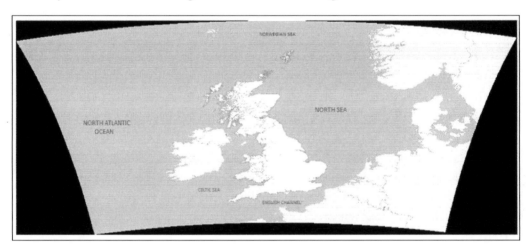

8.   Now that we have our information stored into a spatial table, we can combine it with several other types of data as we did in the previous chapter, as shown in the following screenshot:

This is just the tip of the iceberg of all the fabulous things that you can make using these powerful and open sourced tools, which are available for free. Now it's up to you to use your imagination to generate a lot of great and visually rich solutions by combining these three tools (PostGIS, GDAL, and QGIS). In *Chapter 8, Developing a GIS Web Application*, we will see how to develop web applications in order to give the user a chance to work with the spatial data in a more automatic manner.

Summary

In this chapter, we learned how to insert both raster and vectorial files directly into our database. We used the GDAL library to transform the available data into the data formats that we need, giving us the possibility of using almost any kind of spatial data file that we have available, regardless of the projection and format it was made in (as long as it's available in GDAL).

In the following chapter, we will see how to work with this data in a more efficient way. When we work with regular databases, we use the indexes to help us to get a better performance from the server, especially when we work with thousands or even millions of registers. PostGIS gives us the possibility of creating indexes that will do the same for us with the spatial data tables. We will see how to accelerate our spatial queries using them.

7

Performance Tuning

It's very common for a spatial database to have millions of records; this could cause our queries' performance to decay a lot when even more data is added. This would have a negative impact if we don't have the right strategies in place to deal with this situation. Similar to the approach used for a regular database, we could create indexes that help the DBMS to create strategies to speed up queries. In a spatial approach, we can use indexes as well. In this chapter, we will learn about the following topics:

- Why the spatial indexes in PostGIS are different from the regular indexes
- Creating a spatial index
- Making sure that PostgreSQL uses these indexes where they're necessary
- Tuning PostgreSQL's configuration for PostGIS

Spatial indexes in PostGIS

PostgreSQL supports three types of indexes:

- B-Trees
- R-Trees
- GIST

The third one, GIST, is a type of index that PostGIS uses for GIS data, so all the spatial indexes must be created in this type. **GIST** stands for **Generalized Search Tree**, and is used to index irregular structures, instead of basic data types (such as integers, characters, strings, and so on). The syntax used to build a GIST index for a geometry column is:

```
CREATE INDEX [indexname] ON [tablename] USING GIST ( [geometryfield] );
```

Here, we can use GUI to build a spatial index instead of a command line. In the next section, we will develop a spatial query and run it with and without an index in order to compare the improvement in speed.

Tuning spatial queries

To illustrate how much an index helps to accelerate our spatial query, let's return to our spatial database, Real-World. We have already loaded data from several cities in Great Britain, and at this time we have more than half a million registers saved in our data table. This set of stored records will be good enough for this exercise.

Now, let's develop the spatial query to perform the test. Let's say that we want a query that gives us a list of all the buildings that were one-fourth of a mile from an arbitrary building. To illustrate this, we have chosen the **Royal College of Music** as a reference point without any particular reason. This image will depict this point graphically:

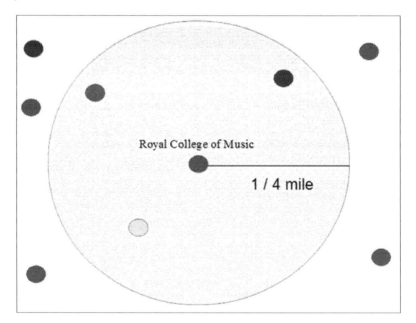

Our spatial query will, therefore, be:

```
SELECT b2.*, ST_Distance(b1.the_geom, b2.the_geom)*69.00 AS distance
FROM tbl_buildings AS b1, tbl_buildings AS b2  WHERE b1.name = 'Royal
College of Music' AND ST_DWithin(b1.the_geom, b2.the_geom, 0.250 /69.00)
```

Let's open a PGAdmin session, copy the query in the SQL editor, and run it. After doing this, you will get a result as shown in the following screenshot:

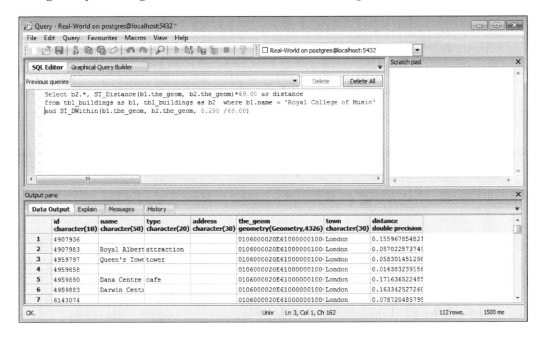

After running the query, we get a result of 112 rows at an elapsed time of 1500 milliseconds. Now, let's generate a spatial index for this table; to do this, we must perform the following steps:

1. In the PGAdmin application, expand the **tbl_buildings** node and go to the **Indexes (0)** node.

2. Right-click on it and in the contextual menu select the **New Index** option:

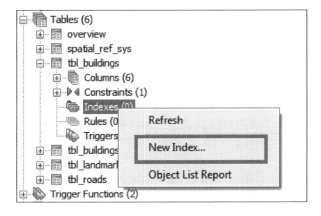

3. In the **New Index...** window, type a name for your index; in this case, we will call it idx_geo_buildings:

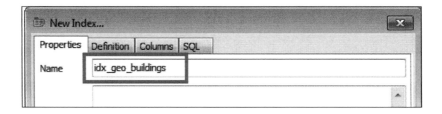

4. Now select the **Definition** tab.

5. It's very important that in the **Access method** combo box, you select the **gist** option:

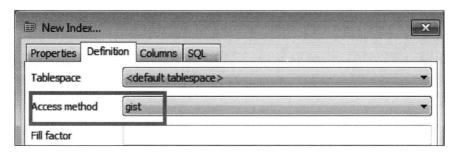

6. Now, let's go to the **Columns** tab; in the **Column** combo box, select the_geom.

7. Click on the **Add** button, as shown in this screenshot:

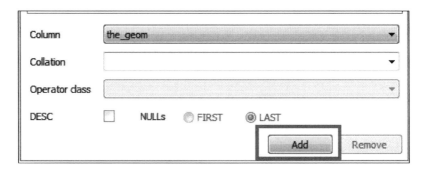

8. Click on the **OK** button for the changes to take effect; it's very probable that this might take a while as PostgreSQL would most likely be generating the index structure at that moment.

9. When the process finishes, you can close the **New Index...** window and see the new index on the indexes list of our table, as shown in this screenshot:

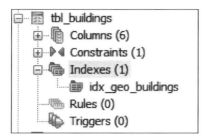

If you prefer, you can generate the index via a command line. To do this, you can type the following command in your **SQL Editor** window:

```
CREATE INDEX idx_geo_buildings ON tbl_buildings USING GIST ( the_geom );
```

Before we can use the index, it is necessary that we vacuum our data table. **Vacuum** is a function that forces PostgreSQL to collect table statistics; this information is later used to optimize queries. In order to vacuum our data table, we must perform the following steps:

1. Right-click on the **tbl_buildings** table icon.

2. In the contextual menu, select the **Maintenance...** option:

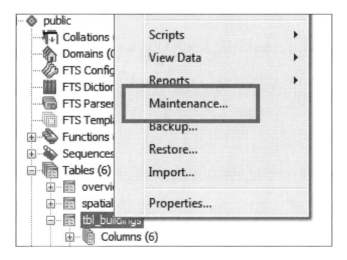

3. In the **Maintenance** window, select **VACUUM**.

4. In the **VACUUM options** section, select the **ANALYZE** option.

5. Click on the **OK** button for the changes to take effect:

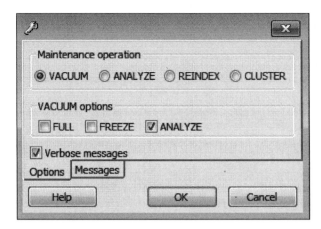

6. When the process finishes, click on the **Done** button:

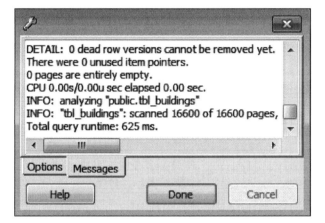

Once again, if you prefer, you can do this process from the command line by running the following command:

```
VACCUM ANALYZE  tbl_buildings (the_geom)
```

Now, let's run our spatial query once again to see whether there are some differences:

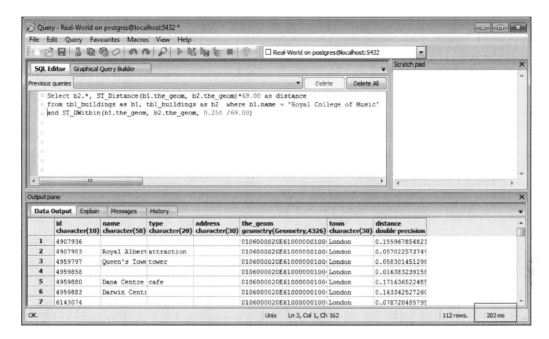

As you can see, the same query takes just 203 milliseconds to take effect, and this is almost eight times faster than before. As you get more registers in your data table, the effect of the spatial index is more notorious; it is very common in the GIS ambit to have tables with millions of registers, so building indexes may be crucial for the project's success in such cases.

There is another important thing that you should know about the usage of spatial indexes. In order to make sure that we make use of these indexes when we run our spatial queries, we must use the EXPLAIN command. This is a command that we put before our query and instead of just running and showing us the result, it runs the query, but also shows us information on how DBMS is running it. Out of the information given to us, it tells us whether the spatial index was used. Now, take a look at this example:

```
EXPLAIN SELECT b2.*, ST_Distance(b1.the_geom, b2.the_geom)*69.00 AS
distance   FROM tbl_buildings AS b1, tbl_buildings AS b2  WHERE b1.name
= 'Royal College of Music' AND ST_DWithin(b1.the_geom, b2.the_geom, 0.250
/69.00);
```

When we run this query, we obtain this result:

```
QUERY PLAN

Nested Loop  (cost=4.34..16628.04 rows=1 width=480)

   -> Seq Scan on tbl_buildings b1  (cost=0.00..16425.05 rows=6
width=164)

          Filter: (name = 'Royal College of Music'::bpchar)

   -> Bitmap Heap Scan on tbl_buildings b2  (cost=4.34..33.78 rows=1
width=316)

          Recheck Cond: (the_geom && st_expand(b1.the_geom,
0.0036231884057971::double precision))

          Filter: ((b1.the_geom && st_expand(the_geom,
0.0036231884057971::double precision)) AND _st_dwithin(b1.the_geom, the_
geom, 0.0036231884057971::double precision))

     -> Bitmap Index Scan on idx_geo_buildings  (cost=0.00..4.34 rows=7
width=0)

              Index Cond: (the_geom && st_expand(b1.the_geom,
0.0036231884057971::double precision))
```

Taking a closer look at the result, we can see that the index has not been used by the DBMS because of the following line:

```
   -> Bitmap Index Scan on idx_geo_buildings  (cost=0.00..4.34 rows=7
width=0)
```

In this case, we are using the ST_DWithin spatial function as a filter. This is a bounding box-based function, which means that it internally constructs a bounding box and uses the && operator. These kinds of functions are the only ones that can actually use the spatial index. Not all spatial functions are bounding box-based, so when you run your query, make sure that your filter function is using it through the EXPLAIN command.

If you are using a bounding box function as a filter and you still find that your spatial indexes are not being used, you can perform the following steps:

1. Run the VACUUM ANALYZE command; this will provide DBMS with better information to make choices about the index usage. Actually, it is a good practice to run this command regularly.

2. If the previous step doesn't work, you can modify the PostgreSQL pertinent parameters, so it will be more probable that DBMS decides to use the index

In the next section, we will see which parameters, and why and how, we can adjust them in order to get a better performance in running the queries.

Tuning PostgreSQL's configuration file for our spatial database

Another important thing that we can do to speed up our database is to adjust some of the parameters that PostgreSQL's DBMS uses. We have to configure new values for them, keeping in mind the specific features of spatial databases (spatial records are usually bigger than nonspatial ones). Now, we will see how to make these changes.

In order to do this, we will have to edit the postgressql.conf file. It's a postgreSQLconfiguration file and we can find it in the C:\Program Files\ PostgreSQL\9.3\data folder.

There are two ways of performing this task; the first is to open it with a text editor, such as Notepad, the second one is to open it using the utility that comes with PGAdmin for these purposes. We can perform the following steps:

1. Run PGAdmin III.
2. Navigate to **File** | postgresql.conf.

3. When the file dialog is opened, navigate to the `C:\Program Files\ PostgreSQL\9.3\data` directory and select the `postgresql.conf` file. You will see a window similar to the following screenshot:

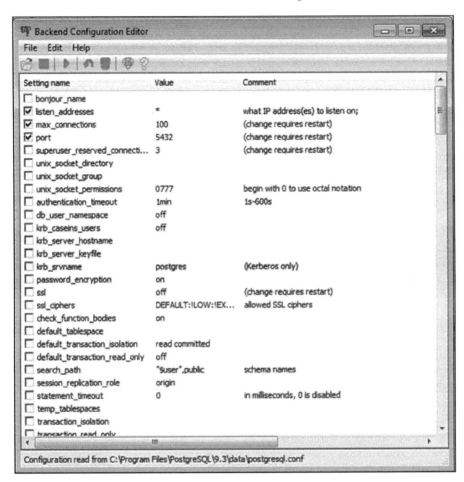

Here, you can graphically change the parameters that rule the behavior of the PostgreSQL database service. These changes will help us to improve the behavior of the database components in order to make it more efficient for the spatial data management. The changes can be the following:

Name	checkpoint_segments
Description	The maximum number of log file segments between automatic WAL checkpoints.
Default value	3

Name	checkpoint_segments
Suggested value	6
Explanation:	Write Ahead Logging (WAL) is a method to ensure that data integrity consists of log changes to the database data (such as tables and indexes) before these changes take effect, so in the case of a database crash, the log can be used to restore it. Therefore, every time that a checkpoint is created, all the data in the memory must be saved to the disk, and this obviously causes a significant I/O load. By incrementing the number of memory segments (typically they are 16 MB in size) that must be filled before a new checkpoint is created, we reduce the workload to our database server. This applies especially well in the case of spatial data records, because they are frequently bigger than the number of spatial pairs, as we mentioned earlier on in this chapter.

Name	constraint_exclusion
Description	This is generally used for table partitioning
Default value	Deactivated
Suggested value	Activated, partition
Explanation:	It will force the planner to only analyze tables for the purpose of constraint consideration if they are in an inherited hierarchy and not pay the planner penalty otherwise

Name	maintenance_work_mem
Description	It defines the amount of memory used for maintenance operations, including vacuuming, index, and foreign key creations.
Default value	16
Suggested value	128
Explanation:	A larger value might improve the performance for vacuuming and restoring databases. Don't set it up larger than this because it can lead to an excess of reserved memory that can affect other processes.

Name	random_page_cost
Description	It represents the cost of a random page access from the disk
Default value	4.0
Suggested value	2.0
Explanation:	Lowering this value will cause it to be more attractive for the system to use index scans on when a query is run

Name	shared_buffers
Description	This sets the amount of memory the database server uses for shared memory buffers
Default value	32 MB
Suggested value	64 MB to 512 MB unlikely for an allocation of more than 40 percent of RAM
Explanation:	Increasing this value from the default usually improves the system performance, but as the PostgreSQL documentation states "The useful range for shared_buffers on Windows systems is generally from 64MB to 512MB"

Name	wal_buffers
Description	It sets the amount of memory used for WAL data.
Default value	64kb
Suggested value	1MB
Explanation:	As mentioned earlier, only once the WAL files have been flushed will the changes be written to the data files themselves. The size of this buffer only needs to be large enough to hold the WAL data for a single typical transaction, because spatial data tends to be larger than nonspatial, and it's recommended to increase the size.

Name	work_mem
Description	It defines the amount of memory that internal sorting operations and hash tables can consume before the database switches to on-disk files
Default value	1MB
Suggested value	16MB
Explanation:	By increasing this value it becomes less probable that the system will run out of available memory for operations (such as ORDER BY and DISTINCT clauses, merge and hash joins, hash-based aggegation and hash-based processing of subqueries), without incurring on-disk writes, which will obviously improve the speed of complex queries

Don't forget that all these values are only suggestions and that you have to find the optimal value according to the needs of your database system. For all the changes to take effect, you must restart the PostgreSQL service.

Summary

In this chapter, you learned how to increase the speed of your spatial queries, something that will be very useful for you when you have tables with millions of registers. We saw the usage of spatial indexes, how to create them in a proper way, and how to force DBMS to use them when a query is fired.

In the next chapter, we will consolidate the learning not only of this chapter, but of the entire book; we will build a GIS application that will use all that we have learned. These kinds of applications are very popular currently as people are in constant touch with this class of technology and want to access all the information they can get. Following the line of this book, we will use open source tools to build the applications. We will once again take up the example of the real-estate company and make two applications: one will be a web application for the customers and the other will be a desktop application to manage data.

8
Developing a GIS Web Application

Now that we have developed our spatial database, the ability to see the data inside it, and actually tuned it to achieve an optimal performance, it's time to develop a useful application, which exploits everything that we have seen in the previous chapters.

When you develop an application, you have to be very clear about who your target audience is; this means thinking about who the users of your application will be and the role of this application in an organization. This fact is crucial when you define not only the application's logic, but also the technology that will support this logic in the best way. We will split the system into two applications:

- **Web application**: Its objective is to be a platform that consumers can use to get information on properties that are available for sale, including the location of them on a map.

- **Desktop application**: The objective of this application is to show a way to manipulate the information on these properties in a visual and easy manner, rather than just using SQL commands to add, remove, or edit data. This information is provided to the managers of a spatial database.

We will use the example of the real estate company to illustrate both these approaches; in this case, we will develop two applications. To provide you with a better understanding, let's describe the roles of the two actors that we will use in the system:

- **Consumer**: A consumer might want information on available properties to see which one fits his or her needs better.

- **Manager**: A manager's prerogative is to be able to manage a property's information (add, remove, or edit it), and especially to set up the geographic position of it in the simplest and most effective way, which will allow him or her to focus on getting the work done.

To explain a system's dynamic nature better, take a look at the following figure:

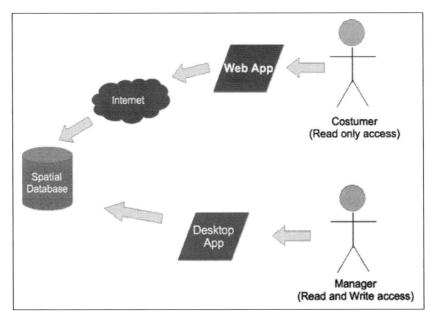

There are a lot of options available when you have to choose the right technology to develop your project. However, it would be impossible to cover all of them in this chapter, though, we will try to cover two of the main development environments you could choose for your application.

We will continue to use open source development tools (such as PHP, JavaScript, and so on), but the examples shown to you will be crafted in a way that will help you adapt them in case you want to use any other commercial language or platform. The purpose of this book isn't to teach you a particular programming language or to configure any web or desktop platform, therefore, we will focus on the interaction with spatial data.

In this chapter, we will cover the following topics:

- Setting up the development environment for a web application using open source tools
- Learning how to create a web application that uses spatial data in our databases

Developing a web application

We can take an example where the management board of the real estate company has decided to add a module to its website where potential clients can check the available properties for sale online. The objective of this is to reinforce the sales process and make the site more attractive and, therefore, the properties must be placed on a map.

You, as chief of the development department, have decided to mount it in a separate server, where you will have an Apache server with a PHP module. In the following sections, we will cover the process that you have to follow in order to achieve the companies' objective; we will touch on some installation aspects of the environment, but in lesser detail, so that we can focus on the development.

Installing the web server

Installing and configuring an Apache web server is not really the objective of this book, so we will cover a very simple and basic installation, which is enough to prepare our environment. If you need more information on installing an Apache web server, you can refer to *Apache Tomcat 7 Essentials*, *Tanuj Khare*, *Packt Publishing* or *PHP Application Development with NetBeans Beginner's Guide*, *M A Hossain Tonu*, *Packt Publishing*. We will assume that you have a Windows machine, actually I will use a Windows 7 computer for the installation, and the process to install it in another version of Windows is also very similar. To do this, perform the following steps:

1. Download the Apache web server from `http://www.apachelounge.com/download/`:

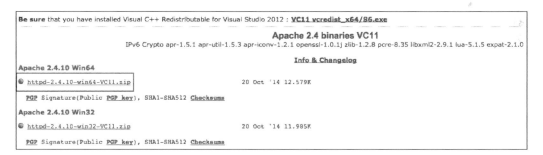

2. Decompress and save it in a machine folder; in this case, we have saved it in `C:\Apache24`. If you choose to install it on a different disk drive (maybe `D:`), you will have to change the `http.conf` file content to redirect the path installation.

3. Open a command line window and execute the following commands:

```
d c:\apache24\bin

httpd.exe -k install
```

This will install `httpd.exe` as a Window's service.

4. Create a shortcut on the desktop to `C:\apache24\bin\ApacheMonitor.exe`. We will run this program to start and stop the web server.

5. Let's probe that everything is okay with the web server; to do this, open your web browser and type: `http://localhost/`. A web page similar to the following screenshot will be displayed:

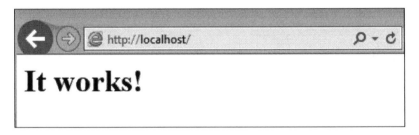

Once we have the web server running, we must install and configure the PHP module in order to generate the scripts that will access our database server. In this case, we choose PHP as a language but you can choose any other and take this example as a reference.

Installing a PHP module

Perform the following steps to install the PHP module:

1. Download the PHP module from `http://windows.php.net/download/`:

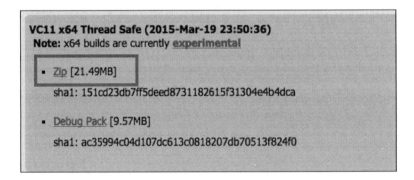

2. Decompress and save it in the machine folder; in this case, we have saved it in `C:\php`.

3. Rename the file from `C:\php\php.ini-production` to `php.in`.

4. Edit the `php.ini` file setting for the following options:

```
doc_root = c:\apache24\htdocs
extension_dir = c:\php\ext
```

5. Go to the extension section and remove the `;` character from the following line:

```
;extension=php_pgsql.dll;
```

This way, you will able to allow PHP to connect to the database server.

6. Open the `C:\apache24\conf\httpd.conf` file and add the following lines at the bottom of the file:

```
LoadModule php5_module "c:/php/php5apache2_4.dll"
AddHandler application/x-httpd-php .php
PHPIniDir "C:/php"
```

7. Save the file and restart the Apache web server, with this command:

```
httpd.exe -k restart
```

8. To probe that everything is working fine, open Notepad and type the following line:

```
<?php phpinfo();?>
```

9. Save it in the `C:\Apache24\htdocs` folder as `test.php`.

10. Now, open your web browser again and load the test script by typing `http://localhost/test.php` on the navigation bar. Once you do this, you will see a page similar to the following screenshot:

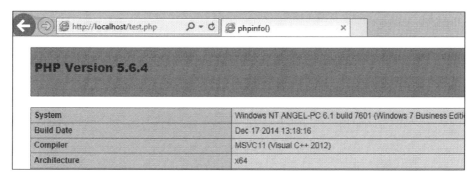

Now that all the underlying services are installed, it's time to install the map visualization component. We have chosen a component that reunites the features of simplicity of usage and beautiful presentation; this component is called **Leaflet**. There are other powerful options, such as OpenLayers and CesiumJS. Packt Publishing books, such as *OpenLayers Cookbook*, *Antonio Santiago Perez* and *OpenLayers 3 Beginner's Guide*, *Thomas Gratier*, *Paul Spencer*, *Erik Hazzard* give you information on these.

Installing Leaflet

Leaflet is a beautiful, light, open source, and free component based on JavaScript; you can find it at `http://leafletjs.com`:

Now, we will see how to install it in order to use it to develop our website. To do this, perform the following steps:

1. Go to the **Download** section.

2. Then, you will have to decompress the download file and copy the content inside the web folder of your server. In this case, we have copied it in `c:\Apache24\htdocs\leaflet`.

Implementing the web application

Now that the component is installed, we can develop our PHP script. We can use the Notepad application to edit it or, if you prefer, any other editing tool, such as Eclipse for PHP, Notepad2, Bluefish Editor, and so on.

Before we start, let's establish the overall structure of the application that we are going to make:

1. First, we will connect our script to the spatial database using PHP.

2. Then, we will create a JavaScript object that will contain the map that the user will see.

3. After this, we will read information on the database and, from it, we will generate the code that will create the necessary JavaScript objects, which will represent the positions of the properties.

We can show this graphically using the following image:

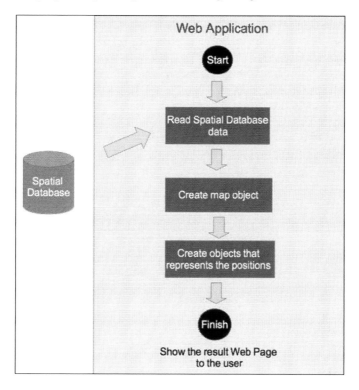

Now, let's start coding our application. Create a file named `index.php` in the `C:\Apache24\htdocs` folder.

First, we must set up the connection to our database server, specifying the connection parameters:

```
// connecting to the database
$dbconnection = pg_connect("host=localhostdbname=Real-Estate
  user=postgres password=123456")       or die('couldn't connect! :
    ' . pg_last_error());
```

Now, let's throw a query to get all the registers saved in the spatial table:

```
$query = 'SELECT id, town, street, number, ST_X(the_geom),
  ST_Y(the_geom) FROM tbl_properties ';
$result = pg_query($query) or die(Query fails!: ' .
  pg_last_error());
```

```php
$line = pg_fetch_row($result);
//We save the position of the first register in those two
  variables
$longitudeView =$line[4];
$latitudeView=$line[5];
```

Let's put some extra attention on the ST_X and ST_Y functions; these extract the x and y values from the geometric object whose values correspond to the longitude and latitude of our spatial position. The purpose of doing this is to obtain the latitude and longitude as separate values; this will allow us to store them on separate variables and then use these variables to create the JavaScript code.

Now, it's time to add the html code of our script. Here, we will add the JavaScript code that we will need to invoke the map component:

```html
<!DOCTYPE html><html><head>
<title>Real Estate Web Page</title>
<meta charset="utf-8" />
<meta name="viewport" content="width=device-width, initial-
  scale=1.0">
<linkrel="stylesheet" href="leaflet/leaflet.css" />
</head><body>
<div id="map" style="width: 600px; height: 400px"></div>
<scriptsrc="leaflet/leaflet.js"></script>
```

Here, we add the link to both the leaflet.css and leaflet.js files that our application will need.

Now, we add the map object; this object will carry one or several layers of information, and each of these layers gives you different kinds of information on the piece of terrain that we are seeing:

```html
<script>
var map = L.map('map');
  L.tileLayer('http://{s}.tile.osm.org/{z}/{x}/{y}.png',
{     attribution: '&copy; <a
  href="http://osm.org/copyright">OpenStreetMap</a> contributors'
    }).addTo(map);
```

In this case, we have added an OpenStreetMap map layer. Here is some PHP code to show the property's position as a marker on the map:

```php
<?php $query = 'SELECT id, town, street, number, ST_X(the_geom),
  ST_Y(the_geom) FROM tbl_properties';
$result = pg_query($query) or die(The query failed: ' .
  pg_last_error());
while ($line =pg_fetch_row($result))
```

```
{
$longitude =$line[4];
$latitude=$line[5];
$address=$line[2]." ".$line[3];
echo "L.marker([".$latitude.", ".$longitude."]).addTo(map)";
echo ".bindPopup('<b>".$address."').openPopup();";
}  ?>
```

We have added code that goes through the table, gives you the position of every piece of property, and generates a market with that position. This market will have a pop-up frame with the address of the property that will be shown when the user clicks on the icon. Later, we will put the map's view as the first property on the table with a zoom level of 16:

```
map.setView([<?php echo $latitudeView.",".$longitudeView ?>], 16);
    </script>
```

Finally, let's draw a table with the data of the properties in it:

```
<?php
// Throwing a query to the properties table
$query = 'SELECT id, town, street, number FROM tbl_properties';
$result = pg_query($query) or die('La consultafallo: ' .
  pg_last_error());
//Printing the results in a html table
echo "<table>\n";
while ($line = pg_fetch_row($result))
{
echo "\t<tr>\n";
echo "\t\t<td><a
  href='index.php?id=".$line[0]."'>".$line[0]."</a></td>\n";
    echo "\t\t<td>".$line[1]."</td>\n";
echo "\t\t<td>".$line[2]."</td>\n";
echo "\t\t<td>".$line[3]."</td>\n";
echo "\t</tr>\n";
}
echo "</table>\n";
//Freeing the result set
pg_free_result($result);
//closing the database connection
pg_close($dbconn);
?>
</body>
</html>
```

As you can see, we have added another cell to the table that contains a hyperlink. This link has the ID of the selected register included as a part of it. This parameter will help us make modifications to the script where it will zoom to the selected property when the user clicks on it.

To get all this implemented we will add the following code at the sixth line of our script:

```
$where="";
if( isset($_GET['id']))
$where=" where id=".$_GET['id'];
```

Now, we will have to modify the query in order to add the `where` clause:

```
$query = 'SELECT id, town, street, number, ST_X(the_geom),
  ST_Y(the_geom) FROM tbl_properties '.$where;
```

Putting everything together, we get the following script:

```
<?php
//Connecting to the database
$dbconn = pg_connect("host=localhostdbname=Real-Estate
  user=postgres password=123456")        or die(Cant connect! '
    .pg_last_error());
$where="";
if( isset($_GET['id']))
$where=" where id=".$_GET['id'];
$query = 'SELECT id, town, street, number, ST_X(the_geom),
  ST_Y(the_geom) FROM tbl_properties '.$where;
$result = pg_query($query) or die(The query failed!! '
  .pg_last_error());
$line = pg_fetch_row($result);
$longitudeView =$line[4];
$latitudeView=$line[5];
?>
<!DOCTYPE html>
<html>
<head>
<title>Real Estate Example</title>
<meta charset="utf-8" />
<meta name="viewport" content="width=device-width, initial-
  scale=1.0">
<linkrel="stylesheet" href="leaflet/leaflet.css" />
</head>
<body>
<div id="map" style="width: 600px; height: 400px"></div>
<scriptsrc="leaflet/leaflet.js"></script>
<script>
```

```
var map = L.map('map');
L.tileLayer('http://{s}.tile.osm.org/{z}/{x}/{y}.png',
{ attribution: '&copy; <a
  href="http://osm.org/copyright">OpenStreetMap</a> contributors'
  }).addTo(map);
<?php
// Throwing a query to the properties table
$query = 'SELECT id, town, street, number, ST_X(the_geom), ST_Y(the_
geom) FROM tbl_properties';
$result = pg_query($query) or die(The query failed!' .
  pg_last_error());
while ($line =pg_fetch_row($result))
{
$longitude =$line[4];
$latitude=$line[5];
$address=$line[2]." ".$line[3];
echo "L.marker([".$latitude.", ".$longitude."]).addTo(map)";
echo ".bindPopup('<b>".$address."').openPopup();";
}
?>
map.setView([<?php echo $latitudeView.",".$longitudeView ?>], 16);
</script>
<?php
// Throwing a query to the properties table
$query = 'SELECT id, town, street, number FROM tbl_properties';
$result = pg_query($query) or die(The query failed! '
  .pg_last_error());
//Printing the results in a html table
echo "<table>\n";
while ($line = pg_fetch_row($result))
{
echo "\t<tr>\n";
echo "\t\t<td><a
  href='index.php?id=".$line[0]."'>".$line[0]."</a></td>\n";
echo "\t\t<td>".$line[1]."</td>\n";
echo "\t\t<td>".$line[2]."</td>\n";
echo "\t\t<td>".$line[3]."</td>\n";
echo "\t</tr>\n"; }
echo "</table>\n";
//Freeing the result set
pg_free_result($result);
// Closing the connection
pg_close($dbconn); ?>
</body>
</html>
```

Now, we open our favorite web browser and see this result:

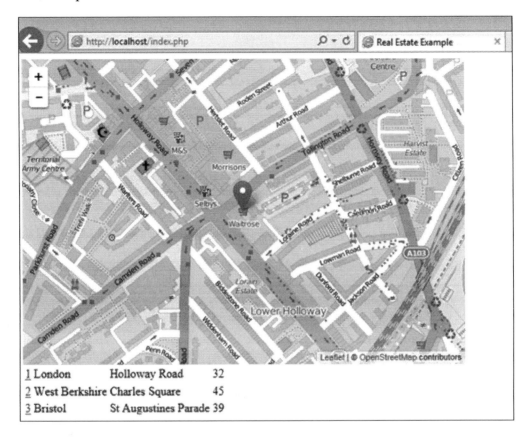

This is just a sample. You can easily add more functionality to the application in case you want to add a private section where you can add extra information for sales people, such as the price of the property, or you might want to add a picture of the house in the pop-up.

Summary

Until now, we have learned how to install and configure an Apache web server with the PHP module enabled and how to use it in conjunction with the Leaflet library to create a web application, which shows the spatial data graphically to a user. For this, we read the information that was already stored in the database; however, you might ask, what if we need to update this information? In the next chapter, we will build a desktop application for managers who can update this information. To achieve this objective, we will use a beautiful and, of course, free and open source SDK called **WorldWind**, which works with Java.

9
Developing a Desktop GIS Application

Following with our sample, you might face a situation where the company asks you to develop an application that can update the information stored in the database. This application will be used just by the staff of a company, which uses different operative systems (Windows, MAC OS, and even Linux), so that the application can run on everyone's system. The reason for this is that the data can be updated by three different people, all of whom use different operative systems.

A good option to use is Java. This is a great and well proofed tool and there is a lot of support for it that you could find freely on the web. You can also buy a good book to find out more on this subject; Packt Publishing has great options, such as *Java EE Development with Eclipse*, *Deepak Vohra* or *Java EE 7 First Look, NDJOBO Armel Fabrice*. However, what do we do about the spatial part? It would prove to be very difficult to set the position of a property without actually seeing it on a map. To do this, we will use a very useful SDK developed by NASA as an open source project called World Wind. In the following subsection, we will learn how to install and develop it and an application that will use it as a tool to show geographic data.

In this chapter, we will cover the following topics:

- Setting up the development environment for a desktop application using open source tools
- Learning to create a desktop application that uses the spatial data stored in our databases

What is World Wind?

World Wind is a **Software Development Kit** (**SDK**) developed in Java and created by NASA as an open source project and is used to craft a GIS application. World Wind uses OpenGL as graphical motor through a binding called **Java Binding for OpenGL** (**JOGL**); this architecture allows World Wind applications to run on several platforms, such as Windows, Linux, and Mac OS.

More precisely, World Wind is a collection of components that interactively display geographic information inside Java applications. These applications use one or more World Wind objects for its user interface. Those objects provide the graphic context in order to be able to show geographic data above a terrestrial globe.

How does World Wind work?

Here, we will show a diagram of the World Wind's object architecture. You can see the main classes that compound World Wind and how they interact with each other:

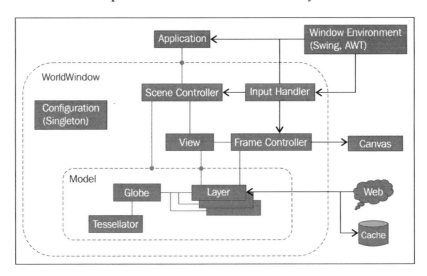

The preceding diagram shows us that the most important class in the World Wind SDK is the **WorldWindow** and it encloses all the functionalities and supporting classes that makes World Wind work. Basically, a **WorldWindow** object is a frame where geographical data is shown. This data is represented by a terrestrial globe. The area of the globe that a user can see at a specific moment is called the **View**; it controls the altitude and the angle that a hypothetical observer must be in, in order to see the terrain in the way that is shown at this time.

Another important class in World Wind is **Layers**. A layer is a set of geographical information (shown as images of the terrain or visual objects) that is shown on the top of the surface of the terrain. As an example, let's say that you have a layer of satellite images from a specific terrain, therefore, on top, you can have a layer that shows the landmarks of a city in the form of icons.

On a typical usage, the applications create a terrestrial globe and add layers of information in order to show their own data; this set of objects is called a Scene. The control of this scene relies on a **WorldWindow** object, which manages the view of the data and its interaction with the user.

World Wind uses the standard **World Map Services (WMS)** to download satellite images; in this case, it comes with several public WMS sources, some of which are provided by NASA itself. You can easily add additional servers that you can access. World Wind automatically downloads the images of the terrain that you're interested in and stores all of them in your local disk. Therefore, if you have downloaded a specific world area when you have access to the Internet, and then you go offline, you will be able to see the images of this terrain repeatedly.

Previous requirements

Now that we have a clearer idea of what World Wind is and how we can use it, we can start installing it on our machine. However, first, let's see the previous hardware and software requirements that need to be fulfilled in order to use it.

Hardware

You can use a Mac (any model that runs MacOS 10.9 or higher version) or a PC with a video card that supports OpenGL 2 or superior versions of it. World Wind has also been proven to work with NVIDIA, ATI/AMD, and Intel cards.

Software

Following are the software requirements:

- World Wind 2.0
- Java JDK 7.0
- Eclipse (for development purposes only)
- Windows, MacOS, or Linux with its graphical drivers correctly installed and updated

Installing World Wind

The process of installing World Wind is actually very easy; all you have to do is to follow a few steps:

1. Open your favorite web browser and go to `http://worldwind.arc.nasa.gov/java/`.

2. Download the most recent and stable version of it; in this case, 2.0:

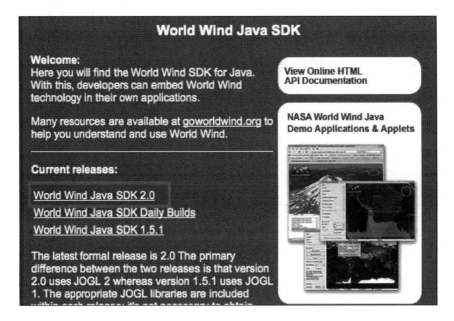

3. Once the download has finished, extract the files in a folder of your choice; this will be the root folder of World Wind. In this case, we have extracted the files in the `My Documents` folder.

4. To check whether everything is okay, open a command line window, go to the World Wind root folder and type the following command:

    ```
    run-demo.bat gov.nasa.worldwindx.examples.ApplicationTemplate
    ```

If everything goes right, you will see the following window:

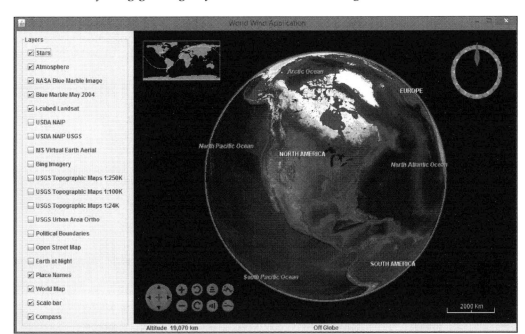

Now that we are sure that World Wind is correctly installed on our machine, we can start configuring the development environment in order to create our own applications.

Setting up the development environment

We have chosen **Eclipse** as a framework. You can select any other one that you like or even use Notepad if you wish to. All you have to know is how to configure the framework you've selected so that it can access the World Wind SDK libraries; in this case, we will show you how to do this in Eclipse. However, we must first install it on our machine.

Installing Eclipse

Eclipse is a very robust and easy-to-use framework and has spent several years on the market, so you may have used it before. It is a very mature open source project that will provide us with a solid developing platform. To install it, perform the following steps:

1. Open your web browser and visit the downloads section of the official web page of the project at `http://www.eclipse.org/downloads`.

2. Select **Eclipse IDE for Java developers** for 64 bits:

Eclipse IDE for Java Developers, 154 MB
Downloaded 585,902 Times

The essential tools for any Java developer, including a Java IDE, a CVS client, Git client, XML Editor, Mylyn, Maven integration...

Windows 32 Bit
Windows 64 Bit

3. Extract the content to any folder on your machine; in this case, we have chosen the `My Documents` folder.

Now, all that you have to do is to execute the `eclipse.exe` file to start the configuration of the development environment.

Configuring the development environment

By configuring the development environment, we will be able to start writing our own applications using the World Wind SDK. To do this, perform the following steps:

1. Execute the `eclipse.exe` files.

2. Select a folder to use as **Workspace**; in this case, select the `My Documents` folder:

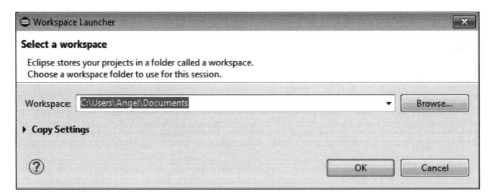

3. Navigate to the **New | Project** from the main menu:

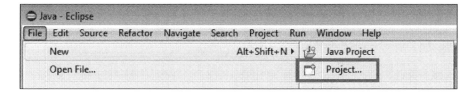

4. Select the **Java Project From existing Ant Buildfile** option and click on the **Next** button:

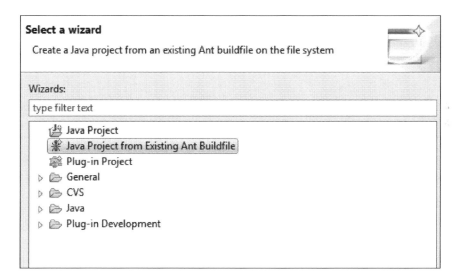

5. In the following window, click on the **Browse...** button that is to the right of the **Ant buildfile** textbox:

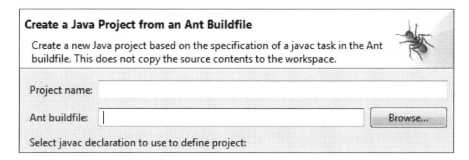

6. Go to the `worldwind` root folder and select the `build.xml` file:

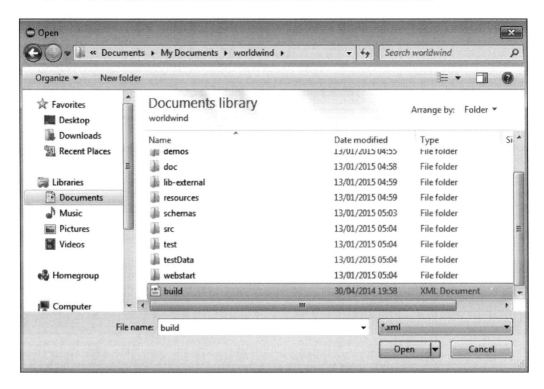

7. Eclipse sets the project name as `worldwind` by default, though you can rename it if you want to; in this case, we will keep it the way it is:

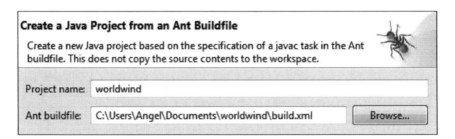

8. Click on the **Finish** button. You will see the following window:

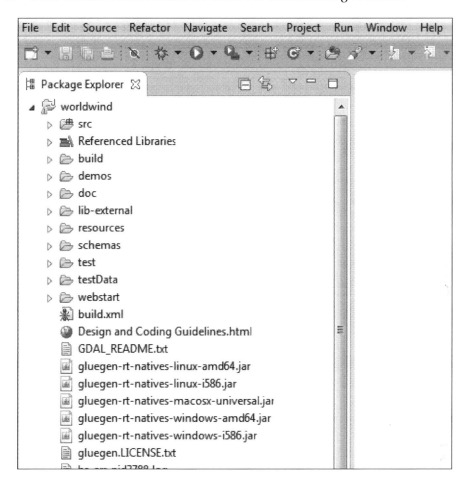

9. As you can see, the World Wind project has several folders with data and demos for testing purposes; the most interesting folder here is the **src** folder, since it contains the entire source code of World Wind and a lot, and I mean a lot, of useful examples. Let's expand and see what's inside it:

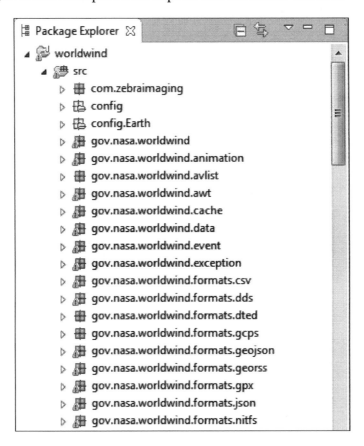

10. There are a lot of packages with classes and subclasses that will provide a lot of spatial functionalities to our applications, simply by adding a reference to this project. Now, let's expand the `gov.nasa.worldwindx.examples` package:

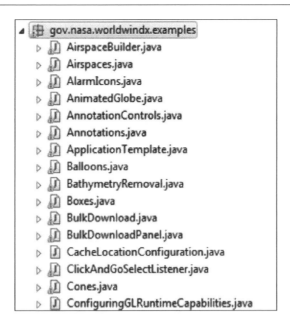

11. You can see here that there are plenty of useful examples that can easily be used as guides to develop the applications we need. Now, to see that everything has been installed and configured properly, let's run an example called `SimplestPossibleExample.java`.

12. To do this we will go to the `SimplestPossibleExample.java` file listed inside the `gov.nasa.worldwindx.examples` package.

13. Right-click on it and navigate to the **Run as | 1 Java Application**, as shown in the following screenshot:

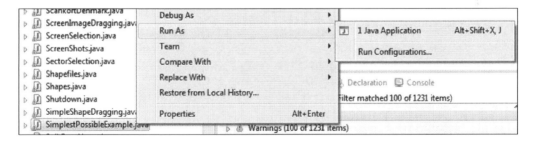

14. If everything is okay, you will see the following window:

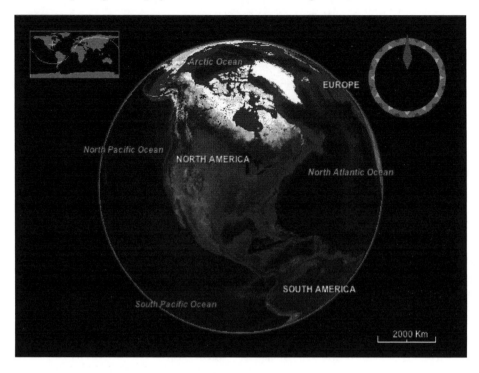

It's great! Now that we are able to run the examples, it's time to make our own test application using SDK. This will reinforce all that we have learned about World Wind in this chapter.

Coding our first application

Let's create a simple application called `HelloWorldWind` that basically will just show the terrestrial globe as the test application of the last subsection; however, the main objective of it is to give us a better understanding of the relationship between the classes and how they must be used when creating an application. To create the test application, perform the following steps:

1. Run Eclipse and navigate to the **File** | **New** | **Java Project**:

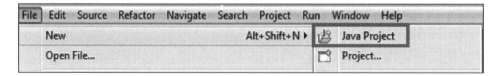

2. Specify the name of the project, in this case, we've chosen `HelloWorldWind`, and then click on the **Finish** button:

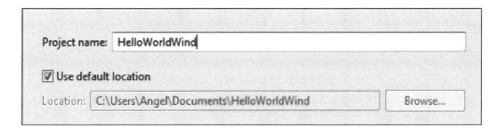

3. Expand the project and right-click on the **src** folder:

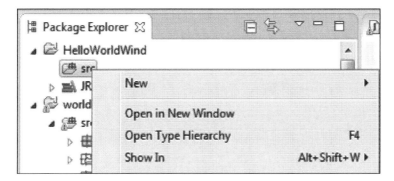

4. Navigate to the **New | Class** as shown in the following screenshot:

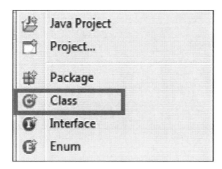

5. In the **Package** textbox, write `Example`, in the class **Name** textbox, write `HelloWorldWind`, in the **Which method stubs would you like to create?** section, check the **public static void main (String args[])** checkbox and click on the **Finish** button:

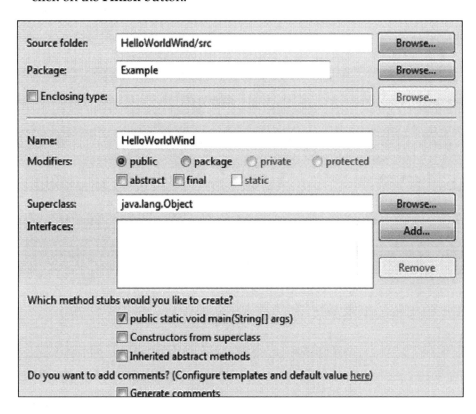

6. If everything is fine, you will see a screen similar to the following screenshot on the editing window of your IDE:

```java
HelloWorldWind.java
1  package Example;
2
3  public class HelloWorldWind {
4
5      public static void main(String[] args) {
6          // TODO Auto-generated method stub
7
8      }
9
10 }
11
```

This tells us that the class was successfully created and it contains a main method that will allow us to run it as a Java application. Now, we must add the World Wind classes that will allow us to transform this simple application into a GIS one! Before we can have access to these classes, we must finish configuring our project in order for it to be able to find the libraries that World Wind uses to run. Let's continue the process by performing the following steps:

1. Right-click on the **HelloWorldWind** project and select the **Properties** option from the contextual menu:

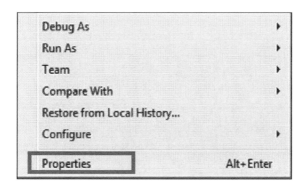

2. Navigate to **Java Build Path | Projects** and click on the **Add...** button:

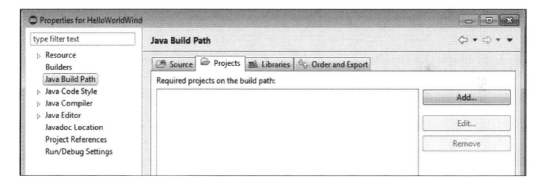

3. In the next window, select the **worldwind** project:

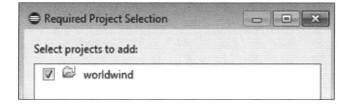

4. Select the **Libraries** tab and click on the **Add External JARs...** button:

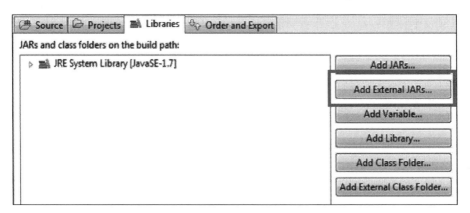

5. Select the `jogl-all` and `glugen-rt` jar files that are inside the `worldwind` root folder:

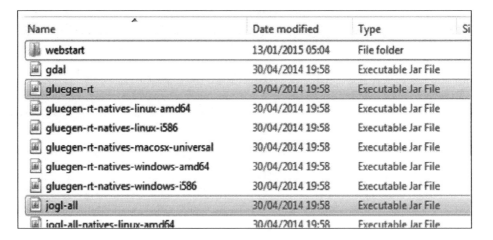

6. Now that you have added the JOGL libraries to the project, click on the **OK** button to finish.

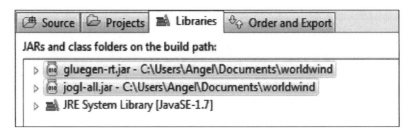

7. Since the project is configured now, let's add some code. The first step is to focus on the window to edit the `HelloWorldWind.jar` file on Eclipse; now we'll add the following code. First, our class must extend the `JFrame` class:

```
public class HelloWorldWind extends JFrame
```

We can see that the IDE detects an error on this code:

8. This is because we have not added the proper reference to this class. Eclipse suggests several possible solutions to fix the error when you click the small bulb, as shown in the following screenshot:

9. In this case, we will add a reference to the suggested class automatically. This is a very common error and we will fix it in this way: in the following code, we will assume that you apply this technique to fix the error:

```
package Example;
import javax.swing.JFrame;

public class HelloWorldWind extends JFrame
{
    public static void main(String[] args) {
        // TODO Auto-generated method stub

    }
}
```

10. Now, we'll add a new object of the `WorldWindowGLCanvas` class called `world` on the 6th line. This object will give you the spatial context, as we saw in the previous sections of this chapter:

```
WorldWindowGLCanvasworld;
```

11. Now, let's create a constructor for our class where we will properly initialize our objects:

```
public HelloWorldWind()
{
   world = new WorldWindowGLCanvas();
   world.setPreferredSize(new java.awt.Dimension(1000,
     800));
   this.getContentPane().add(world,
     java.awt.BorderLayout.CENTER);
   world.setModel(new BasicModel());
}
```

12. The `BasicModel` class adds the globe of the earth and the default information layers to the `WorldWindow` context. Now, in line 21, we'll add the following code:

```
java.awt.EventQueue.invokeLater(new Runnable()
{
public void run()
{
JFrame frame = new HelloWorldWind();
frame.setDefaultCloseOperation(JFrame.EXIT_ON_CLOSE);
frame.setName("My first Application");
frame.pack();
frame.setVisible(true);
}
});
```

13. This simply allows the class that we crafted earlier to run. Putting everything together, we get the following code:

```
import gov.nasa.worldwind.BasicModel;
import gov.nasa.worldwind.awt.WorldWindowGLCanvas;
import javax.swing.JFrame;
public class HelloWorldWind extends JFrame
{
WorldWindowGLCanvas world;
public HelloWorldWind()
{
world = new WorldWindowGLCanvas();
world.setPreferredSize(new java.awt.Dimension(1000, 800));
   this.getContentPane().add(world,
   java.awt.BorderLayout.CENTER);  world.setModel(new
     BasicModel());
}
```

```
public static void main(String[] args)
{
// TODO Auto-generated method stub
  java.awt.EventQueue.invokeLater(new Runnable()
{
public void run()
{
JFrame frame = new HelloWorldWind();
    frame.setDefaultCloseOperation(JFrame.EXIT_ON_CLOSE);
    frame.setName("My first Application");
    frame.pack();
    frame.setVisible(true);
}
});
}
}
```

14. Now, run the code in the same way that you did in the World Wind example; you will then see the following window:

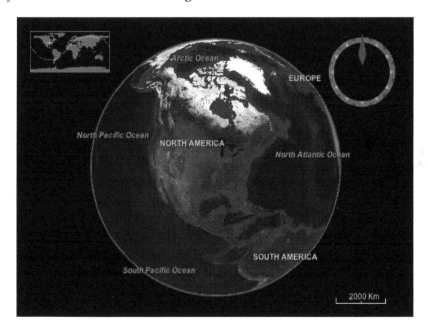

Now that we have successfully developed and built our first application using World Wind, we are almost ready to start the final application, but before this, we have to find a way to communicate our application with the database. For this purpose, we must get the PostgreSQL–Java binding so that we can connect the application to the database and run all the necessary queries.

Getting the PostgreSQL–Java binding

The PostgreSQL-Java binding is a library, which is in the form of a `.jar` file that we need so that our application can establish a connection with the database. We will now see the steps to follow to get this library:

1. Open your web browser and go to `https://jdbc.postgresql.org/download.html`.

2. Download the **JDBC3 PostgreSQL Driver, Version 9.3-1102** file:

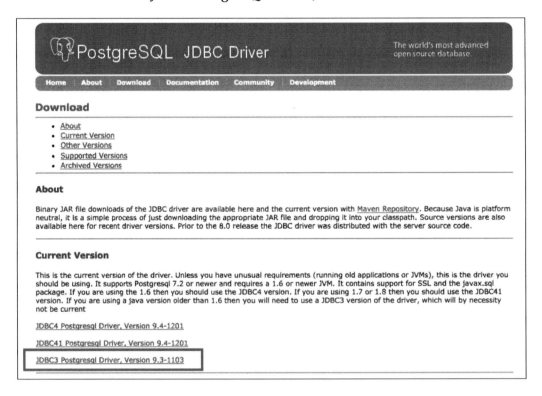

Once it's downloaded, you will have to add this file to your Java project as an external `jar`, similar to what was done in previous sections of this chapter. To make sure that the library works properly on our machine, let's develop an example application. To do this, follow these steps:

3. Run Eclipse.

4. Create a new project called `Hello_PostgreSQL`.

5. Create a class called `testPostgreSQL`.

6. Add the `postgresql-9.3-1102.jdbc3.jar` file as an external jar to your project.

7. Add the following code:

```java
import java.sql.Connection;
import java.sql.DriverManager;
import java.sql.ResultSet;
import java.sql.SQLException;
import java.sql.Statement;
public class testPostgreSQL
{
  public static void main(String[] args)
  {
    // TODO Auto-generated method stub
    Connection connnection = null;
    Statement statement = null;
    ResultSet rs = null;
    String url = "jdbc:postgresql://localhost/Real-Estate";
    String user = "postgres";
    String password = "123456";
    try
    {
      connnection = DriverManager.getConnection(url, user,
        password);
      statement = connnection.createStatement();
      rs = statement.executeQuery("SELECT VERSION()");
      if (rs.next())
      {
        System.out.println(rs.getString(1));
      }
    }
    catch (SQLException ex)
    {
      ex.printStackTrace();
    }
    finally
    {
      try
      {
        if (rs != null)
        {
          rs.close();
        }
        if (statement != null)
        {
          statement.close();
        }
```

```
            if (connnection != null)
            {
              connnection.close();
            }
          }
          catch (SQLException ex)
          {
            ex.printStackTrace();
          }
        }
      }
    }
```

8. Let's run the project; we must obtain an output similar to this:

```
PostgreSQL 9.3.5, compiled by Visual C++ build 1600, 64-bit
```

Now we are ready to start developing our final application. We will follow and step-by-step style the developing, but for now, we will make more assumptions about the management of the IDE, so that we can focus on developing the spatial objects.

Developing a management application

Taking the example of the real estate company again, we have to develop a software module that will allow administrators to manage (add, edit, and erase) the information (including the geographic position) of the properties that the company has available for sale. This application should enable the user to specify the data of a property and set its position on a map by clicking on the terrain. This data must be stored in the database in the form of geographic data.

Let's begin this process; follow these steps and keep the lessons that you've learned in the past in mind, because we will focus on the development:

1. Create a new project called `Real_Estate_Managment`.
2. Set up the project adding the necessary libraries.
3. Create a class called `Main` that extends `JFrame` and includes the `public.static.main` method.
4. Declare a `WorldWindowGLCanvas` object called `world`.
5. Create a constructor where you initialize the window and the world objects, as we did in the `HelloWorldWind` application.

6. We will declare a new object from the `Layer` class called `propertiesLayer` and initialize it on the constructor in the following code snippet. This object will hold all the icons that will represent the properties on the map:

```
propertiesLayer = new RenderableLayer();
```

7. Below this line, create a new object of the `LayerList` class called `layers` and initialize it on the constructor. The layers object holds the set of layers included on the world object. This collection will allow us to add new layers or remove existing ones:

```
LayerList layers = world.getModel().getLayers();
```

Now that the main World Wind objects are set, let's create a set of objects that will allow us to connect to the PostgreSQL server. To do this, perform the following steps:

1. Create a new `Java.sql.connection` object called `Connection`.

2. In the constructor, let's initialize it and add a `Statement` and a `Resultset` object as we did on the `testPostgreSQL` project:

```
connection = null;
Statement statement = null;
ResultSet resultset = null;
```

3. Let's create string variables to hold the connection parameters:

```
String url = "jdbc:postgresql://localhost/Real-Estate";
String user = "postgres";
String password = "123456";
```

4. Create the `connection` and the `statement` objects using the parameters of the previous step:

```
connection= DriverManager.getConnection(url, user, password);
statement= connexion.createStatement();
```

5. Now, we will create a query that procures the data from the `properties` table:

```
resultset = statement.executeQuery("SELECT id, town,
  street, number, ST_X(the_geom), ST_Y(the_geom) FROM
    tbl_properties");
```

6. Now, let's go through the received records to add an icon that represents the position of one of the properties:

```
while (resultset.next())
{
PointPlacemarkplacemark = new
  PointPlacemark(Position.fromDegrees
    (resultset.getDouble(6), resultset.getDouble(5), 0));
placemark.setLabelText(resultset.getString(3)+"
  "+resultset.getString(4));propertiesLayer.addRenderable
    (placemark);
}
```

The `PointPlacemark` class allows us to insert an icon on the surface of the map. We have to add this object to a layer through the `addRendereable` method, so that it can be viewed by the user.

7. Close both the `statement` and the `resultset` objects:

```
if (resultset != null)
{
   resultset.close();
}
if (statement != null)
{
   statement.close();
}
```

8. Let's add a line where the layer that contains the position of the properties will be added to the set of layers that the `world` object contains:

```
layers.add(propertiesLayer);
```

9. Now, put the necessary code to run the application inside the main method, taking the `HelloWorldWind` example as a guide, and substituting the name of the class and the title of the application:

```
java.awt.EventQueue.invokeLater(new Runnable()
{
public void run()
{
JFrame frame = new Main();
frame.setDefaultCloseOperation(JFrame.EXIT_ON_CLOSE);
frame.setName("Managment Application");
frame.pack();
frame.setVisible(true);
}
});
```

10. Now, we'll run the application and see this result:

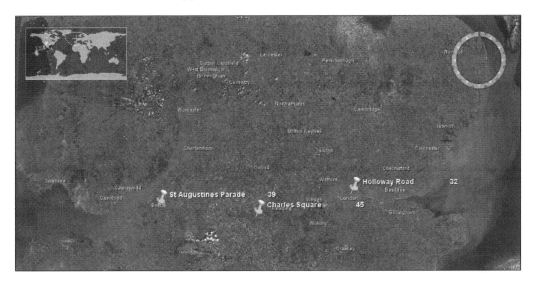

There are a lot of things to be changed, but this a good start. The first thing that I would like to change is the default position of the view of Earth. It would be nice if the first thing that the user sees in the map is that the first property is in the table.

Now, we'll create a procedure that changes the position of the point of view of the observer:

```
private void changeView(double latitude, double longitude)
{
  Position centerPosition = new
    Position(Angle.fromDegrees(latitude),
  Angle.fromDegrees(longitude), 1000);
  world.getView().setEyePosition(centerPosition);
  world.redraw();
}
```

This procedure will set the point of view at the indicated position at an altitude of 1000 meters. We can call this procedure when we are reading the records; in this case, let's take just the first record of the table:

```
if(i == 0)
{
    changeView(resultset.getDouble(6), resultset.getDouble(5));
}
 i++;
```

Now, what if you want to change the yellow pin for something else? Well, you can achieve this by adding the following lines:

```
PointPlacemarkAttributes attributes = new PointPlacemarkAttributes();
attributes.setImageAddress("images\\pushpins\\castshadow-
    green.png");
```

This object is a modifier that allows us to change several properties of the `placemark` objects, among which is the image that it shows. For this to take effect, you just have to add the following line of code when you create the `placemarks`:

```
placemark.setAttributes(attributes);
```

Back to our main objective, we need a window where the user can see and edit the data stored in the database, because of this, we have created a new frame class called `ManagementWindow` that includes a data table to see all the records that are stored:

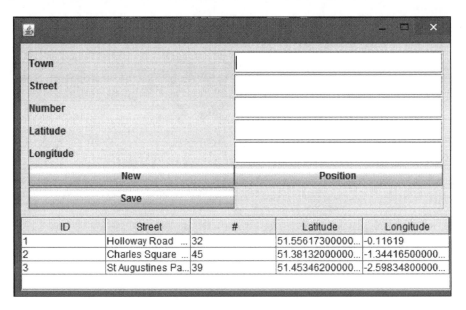

When you click on a row of the table, the data is shown in the textboxes. Since this part of the code is not relative to the spatial data, explaining it is beyond this book's objective and will be obviated.

An interesting functionality that our application must cover is the ability to catch the position of a click on the map when the user asks it. In this case, this position must be caught after the user clicks on the **Position** button. The position value must appear on the latitude and longitude textboxes. To achieve this, we first must go to the `Main.java` file and add this procedure:

```
private void AddPositionListener()
{
  this.world.getInputHandler().addMouseListener(new MouseAdapter()
  {
    public void mousePressed(MouseEvent mouseEvent)
    {
      if (armed && mouseEvent.getButton() == MouseEvent.BUTTON1)
      {
        Position curPos = world.getCurrentPosition();
        if (curPos != null)
        {
          armed=false;
        }
        mouseEvent.consume();
      }
    }
  }
  );
}
```

This procedure uses a flag called `armed`, and it will be fired when the user clicks on the **Position** button. On every window, we will need a link to point to each other. This has been explained as follows:

On the `Main.jar` file:

```
ManagementWindow mwindow;
```

At the end of the constructor:

```
mwindow = new ManagementWindow(this);
mwindow.setVisible(true);
```

On the `ManagementWindow.jar` file:

```
Main mainWindow;
```

In the constructor:

```
this.mainWindow = mainWindow;
```

We have to add a public method in the ManagementWindow that allows you to change the value of the latitude and longitude textboxes:

```
public void setPositionInTextBoxes(double latitude, double
  longitude)
{
  tfLatitude.setText(Double.toString(latitude));
  tfLongitude.setText(Double.toString(longitude));
}
```

In the AddPositionListener method, we can add these lines:

```
if (curPos != null)
{
  armed=false;
  mwindow.setPositionInTextBoxes(curPos.getLatitude().degrees,
  curPos.getLongitude().degrees);
}
```

Finally, add a method that creates the query that inserts the data (including the spatial data, of course) into the database:

```
private String createInsertionQuery()
{
  String query;
  query = "Insert into tbl_properties (town, street, number,
    the_geom) "+
"values ('" +tfTown.getText()+ "', '" +tfStreet.getText()+ "', "
  +tfNumber.getText()+ ", "+
  "ST_GeomFromEWKT('SRID=4623;POINT("+tfLongitude.getText()+"
    "+tfLatitude.getText()+" )') ) ";
  return query;
}
```

All that we have to do is to call this function when the user clicks on the **Save** button. Let's put everything together and see the entire code of both the windows:

```
Main.java
import java.awt.event.MouseAdapter;
import java.awt.event.MouseEvent;
import java.sql.Connection;
import java.sql.DriverManager;
import java.sql.ResultSet;
```

```java
import java.sql.SQLException;
import java.sql.Statement;
import gov.nasa.worldwind.BasicModel;
import gov.nasa.worldwind.awt.WorldWindowGLCanvas;
import gov.nasa.worldwind.geom.Angle;
import gov.nasa.worldwind.geom.Position;
import gov.nasa.worldwind.layers.LayerList;
import gov.nasa.worldwind.layers.RenderableLayer;
import gov.nasa.worldwind.render.PointPlacemark;
import gov.nasa.worldwind.render.PointPlacemarkAttributes;
import javax.swing.JFrame;
public class Main extends JFrame
{
  //declaration of the objects that we will need
  WorldWindowGLCanvas world;
  RenderableLayer propertiesLayer;
  Connection connection;
  boolean armed =false;
  ManagementWindow mwindow;
  public Main()
  {
    //initializing the "world window component"
    world = new WorldWindowGLCanvas();
    world.setPreferredSize(new java.awt.Dimension(1000, 800));
    this.getContentPane().add(world,
      java.awt.BorderLayout.CENTER);
    world.setModel(new BasicModel());
    //its necessary to create this object to set some visual
      //properties to the placemarks
    PointPlacemarkAttributes attributes = new
      PointPlacemarkAttributes();
    attributes.setImageAddress("images\\pushpins\\castshadow-
      green.png");
    //on this layer we will set put the icons that represents the
      //properties
    propertiesLayer  = new RenderableLayer();
    //its necessary to obtain a layer list to add a new layer
    LayerList layers = world.getModel().getLayers();
    //Those objects help us to connect to the database
    connection = null;
    Statement statement = null;
    ResultSet resultset = null;
    //those are the connection parameters
    String url = "jdbc:postgresql://localhost/Real-Estate";
```

```
String user = "postgres";
String password = "123456";
try
{
  //we set the connection with the database
  connection = DriverManager.getConnection(url, user,
    password);
  statement = connection.createStatement();
  //now we throw a query to obtain the positions
  resultset = statement.executeQuery("SELECT id, town, street,
    number, ST_X(the_geom), ST_Y(the_geom) FROM
      tbl_properties");
  int i=0;
  //its necessary to go thru all the registers
  while (resultset.next())
  {
  //we will create an new visual object for every property and
  //add it to the visuallayer that we have created earlier
  PointPlacemark placemark = new
    PointPlacemark(Position.fromDegrees
      (resultset.getDouble(6), resultset.getDouble(5), 0));
  //the placemark will have a label with the address of the
    property
  placemark.setLabelText(resultset.getString(3)+"
    "+resultset.getString(4));
  placemark.setAttributes(attributes);
  propertiesLayer.addRenderable(placemark);
  //we change the view to focus just to the position of the
    first //property on the table
  if(i == 0)
  {
    changeView(resultset.getDouble(6),
      resultset.getDouble(5));
    }
    i++;
  }
}
catch(Exception ex)
{
  ex.printStackTrace();
}
finally
{
//its necessary to close the connection to the batabase
try {
```

```
    if (resultset != null)
    {
      resultset.close();
    }
    if (statement != null)
    {
      statement.close();
    }
  }
  catch (SQLException ex)
  {
    ex.printStackTrace();
  }
}
//now we add the layer that we have created to the layer list
layers.add(propertiesLayer);
//this window will bring the user the GUI for he can edit the
  data
mwindow = new ManagementWindow(this);
mwindow.setVisible(true);
//we have added and event to "hear" when the mouse clicks the
  screen
AddPositionListener();
}
//this function change the point of view of the observer
public void changeView(double latitude, double longitude)
{
  Position centerPosition = new
    Position(Angle.fromDegrees(latitude),
  Angle.fromDegrees(longitude), 1000);
  world.getView().setEyePosition(centerPosition);
  world.redraw();
}
//this is a flag that allows that the geographic position of the
  //mouse click on the screen can be stored when its active
public void setArmed(boolean armed)
{
  this.armed =armed;
}
//returns the own connection to the database
public Connection getConnection()
{
  return connection;
}
```

```
//this method help us to catch the position from the screen on
  //latitude, logitude
private void AddPositionListener()
{
  //this way the handler has more priority that the default
    windo //handler
  this.world.getInputHandler().addMouseListener(new
    MouseAdapter()
  {
    public void mousePressed(MouseEvent mouseEvent)
    {
      if (armed && mouseEvent.getButton() == MouseEvent.BUTTON1)
      {
        Position curPos = world.getCurrentPosition();
        if (curPos != null)
        {
          armed=false;
          //just where everything goes OK the position must be
            represented
              mwindow.setPositionInTextBoxes
                (curPos.getLatitude().degrees,
                  curPos.getLongitude().degrees);
          }
          mouseEvent.consume();
          }
        }
      }
      );
  }
  //sneds the new position to the GUI components
  private void addPosition()
  {
    Position curPos = this.world.getCurrentPosition();
    if (curPos != null)
    {
      //this function makes the trick
      mwindow.setPositionInTextBoxes
        (curPos.getLatitude().degrees,
          curPos.getLongitude().degrees);
      armed=false;
    }
  }
  public static void main(String[] args) {
  // TODO Auto-generated method stub
```

```
      java.awt.EventQueue.invokeLater(new Runnable()
      {
        public void run()
        {
          JFrame frame = new Main();
          //Runs the application
            frame.setDefaultCloseOperation
              (JFrame.EXIT_ON_CLOSE);
          frame.setName("Managment Application");
          frame.pack();
          frame.setVisible(true);
          }
      });
    }
}
ManagementWindow.jar
import gov.nasa.worldwind.geom.Position;
import java.awt.BorderLayout;
import java.awt.Dimension;
import java.awt.GridLayout;
import java.awt.event.ActionEvent;
import java.awt.event.ActionListener;
import java.sql.ResultSet;
import java.sql.SQLException;
import java.sql.Statement;
import javax.swing.BorderFactory;
import javax.swing.JButton;
import javax.swing.JFrame;
import javax.swing.JLabel;
import javax.swing.JPanel;
import javax.swing.JScrollPane;
import javax.swing.JTable;
import javax.swing.JTextField;
import javax.swing.ListSelectionModel;
import javax.swing.border.CompoundBorder;
import javax.swing.border.TitledBorder;
import javax.swing.event.ListSelectionEvent;
import javax.swing.event.ListSelectionListener;
import javax.swing.table.AbstractTableModel;
import javax.swing.table.DefaultTableModel;
public class ManagementWindow extends JFrame
{
  //objects for the communication to the database and the
    graphical //visualization
```

```java
DefaultTableModel  tableModel;
Main mainWindow;
Statement st = null;
ResultSet rs = null;
private Object[] row;
JTextField tfTown ;
JTextField tfStreet;
JTextField tfNumber;
JTextField tfLatitude ;
JTextField tfLongitude;
//new register
boolean isNewRow=true;
public ManagementWindow(Main mainWindow1)
{
  //sets the window dimention
  this.mainWindow = mainWindow1;
  setAlwaysOnTop(true);
  setLocation(0, 300);
  setSize(400, 300);
  //sets all the necessary GUI components
  JPanel panelTop = new JPanel(new GridLayout(0, 2, 0,
    1));
  panelTop.setBorder( new
    CompoundBorder(BorderFactory.createEmptyBorder(9, 9,
      9, 9), new TitledBorder("")));
  panelTop.setToolTipText("Data");
  this.add(panelTop, BorderLayout.NORTH);
  panelTop.add(new JLabel("Town", JLabel.LEFT));
  tfTown = new JTextField(20);
  panelTop.add(tfTown);
  JLabel label1 = new JLabel("Street", JLabel.LEFT);
  panelTop.add(label1);
  tfStreet = new JTextField(20);
  panelTop.add(tfStreet);
  panelTop.add(new JLabel("Number", JLabel.LEFT));
  tfNumber = new JTextField(20);
  panelTop.add(tfNumber);
  panelTop.add(new JLabel("Latitude", JLabel.LEFT));
  tfLatitude = new JTextField(20);
  panelTop.add(tfLatitude);
  panelTop.add(new JLabel("Longitude", JLabel.LEFT));
  tfLongitude = new JTextField(20);
  panelTop.add(tfLongitude);
  JButton btnNuevo = new JButton("New");
```

```
btnNuevo.addActionListener(new ActionListener() {
  //when you click the "New" button al, the text will
    dissapear
  @Override
  public void actionPerformed(ActionEvent arg0)
  {
    isNewRow=true;
    clearDataInTextBoxes();
  }
});
panelTop.add(btnNuevo);
JButton btnPosition = new JButton("Position");
btnPosition.addActionListener(new ActionListener() {
  //when you click the position button you are activating
    the flags //to catch the position of the mouse into
      the terrain
  @Override
  public void actionPerformed(ActionEvent arg0)
  {
    ManagementWindow.this.mainWindow.setArmed(true);
  }
});
panelTop.add(btnPosition);
JButton btnSave = new JButton("Save");
btnSave.addActionListener(new ActionListener() {
  //here the data that the user entered will be saved
  @Override
  public void actionPerformed(ActionEvent arg0)
  {
    String query = createInsertionQuery();
    try {
      st = mainWindow.getConnection().createStatement();
      rs = st.executeQuery(query);
    } catch (SQLException e) {
      // TODO Auto-generated catch block
      e.printStackTrace();
    }
  }
});
panelTop.add(btnSave);
tableModel = new DefaultTableModel ();
//here we will set the columns names
String[] columnNames = {"ID",
  "Street",
```

```
  "#",
  "Latitude",
"Longitude"};
//sets the visual names of the columns
tableModel.setColumnIdentifiers(columnNames);
try {
  st = mainWindow.getConnection().createStatement();
  //here the query that brings all the porperties on the
    table is //runned
  rs = st.executeQuery("SELECT id, town, street, number,
  ST_X(the_geom), ST_Y(the_geom) FROM tbl_properties");
  while (rs.next())
  {
    //we will fill out datatable
    System.out.println(rs.getString(5));
    String[] data = new String[5];
    data[0] = rs.getString(1);
    data[1] = rs.getString(3);
    data[2] = rs.getString(4);
    data[3] = rs.getString(6);
    data[4] = rs.getString(5);
    tableModel.addRow(data);
  }
} catch (SQLException e) {
  // TODO Auto-generated catch block
  e.printStackTrace();
}
//visual components to show the table content
JTable table = new JTable(tableModel);
table.setPreferredScrollableViewportSize(new
  Dimension(500, 70));
table.setFillsViewportHeight(true);
JScrollPane scrollPane = new JScrollPane(table);
add(scrollPane);
table.setSelectionMode
  (ListSelectionModel.SINGLE_SELECTION);
ListSelectionModel selectionModel =
  table.getSelectionModel();
selectionModel.addListSelectionListener(new
  ListSelectionListener() {
//when a row of the table is selected this event is fired
public void valueChanged(ListSelectionEvent e)
{
  handleSelectionEvent(e);
}
```

```
    });
}
//cleans all the data on the databoxes
public void clearDataInTextBoxes()
{
  tfTown.setText("");
  tfStreet.setText("");
  tfNumber.setText("");
  setPositionInTextBoxes(0, 0);
}
//creates the insertion query getting the data fron the visual
  //componets
private String createInsertionQuery()
{
  String query;
  query = "Insert into tbl_properties (town, street, number,
    the_geom) "+"values ('" +tfTown.getText()+ "', '"
      +tfStreet.getText()+ "', " +tfNumber.getText()+ ", "+
    " ST_GeomFromEWKT('SRID=4623;POINT
      ("+tfLongitude.getText()+"
        "+tfLatitude.getText()+" )') ) ";
  return query;
}
//stablish the data that must be showed on the textboxes
public void setDataInTextBoxes(String town, String street,
  String number,
double latitude, double longitude)
{
  isNewRow = false;
  tfTown.setText(town);
  tfStreet.setText(street);
  tfNumber.setText(number);
  setPositionInTextBoxes(latitude, longitude);
}
//sets the right textboxes with the position data
public void setPositionInTextBoxes(double latitude, double
  longitude)
{
  tfLatitude.setText(Double.toString(latitude));
  tfLongitude.setText(Double.toString(longitude));}
  //when the user select a row this code will be fired and the
    data //stored on that row will be showed on the GUI
      components
  protected void handleSelectionEvent(ListSelectionEvent e) {
    if (e.getValueIsAdjusting())
```

```
    return;
    String strSource= e.getSource().toString();
    int start = strSource.indexOf("{")+1,
    stop  = strSource.length()-1;
    String numrow = (strSource.substring(start, stop));
    String town =
      (String)tableModel.getValueAt(Integer.parseInt(numrow),
        0);
    String street =
      (String)tableModel.getValueAt(Integer.parseInt(numrow),
        1);
    String number =
      (String)tableModel.getValueAt(Integer.parseInt(numrow),
        2);
    String latitudeString =
      (String)tableModel.getValueAt(Integer.parseInt(numrow),
        3);
    String longitudeString =
      (String)tableModel.getValueAt(Integer.parseInt(numrow),
        4);
    double latitude = Double.parseDouble(latitudeString);
    double longitude = Double.parseDouble(longitudeString);
    mainWindow.changeView(latitude, longitude);
    setDataInTextBoxes(town, street, number, latitude,
      longitude);
  }
}
```

As you can see, the application is not fully finished yet. I will let you finish this. As an example, you can easily add functionalities to modify and delete the data, or maybe you would like to set a field to specify an image icon for every property.

Summary

In this chapter, you learned how to develop a desktop application using PostGIS. To do this, we used the World Wind SDK, which has a tremendous amount of useful spatial functions that could definitely help us build a much more complex application than this one. It will be very difficult, if not impossible, to cover all the possible options that you have when developing applications that have similar characteristics, in a single book. I believe that the samples that we developed throughout this book will serve as a guide for you if you choose or are familiar with any other development tool.

I sincerely hope that this book has fulfilled your expectations and necessities. I hope that this was just the beginning of a very long and productive relationship between you and PostGIS and that this book has contributed toward it. Thanks a lot.

Index

Thank you for buying
PostGIS Essentials

About Packt Publishing

Packt, pronounced 'packed', published its first book, *Mastering phpMyAdmin for Effective MySQL Management*, in April 2004, and subsequently continued to specialize in publishing highly focused books on specific technologies and solutions.

Our books and publications share the experiences of your fellow IT professionals in adapting and customizing today's systems, applications, and frameworks. Our solution-based books give you the knowledge and power to customize the software and technologies you're using to get the job done. Packt books are more specific and less general than the IT books you have seen in the past. Our unique business model allows us to bring you more focused information, giving you more of what you need to know, and less of what you don't.

Packt is a modern yet unique publishing company that focuses on producing quality, cutting-edge books for communities of developers, administrators, and newbies alike. For more information, please visit our website at www.packtpub.com.

About Packt Open Source

In 2010, Packt launched two new brands, Packt Open Source and Packt Enterprise, in order to continue its focus on specialization. This book is part of the Packt Open Source brand, home to books published on software built around open source licenses, and offering information to anybody from advanced developers to budding web designers. The Open Source brand also runs Packt's Open Source Royalty Scheme, by which Packt gives a royalty to each open source project about whose software a book is sold.

Writing for Packt

We welcome all inquiries from people who are interested in authoring. Book proposals should be sent to author@packtpub.com. If your book idea is still at an early stage and you would like to discuss it first before writing a formal book proposal, then please contact us; one of our commissioning editors will get in touch with you.

We're not just looking for published authors; if you have strong technical skills but no writing experience, our experienced editors can help you develop a writing career, or simply get some additional reward for your expertise.

PostgreSQL Administration Essentials

ISBN: 978-1-78398-898-3   Paperback: 142 pages

Discover efficient ways to administer, monitor, replicate, and handle your PostgreSQL databases

1. Learn how to detect bottlenecks and make sure your database systems offer superior performance to your end users.

2. Replicate your databases to achieve full redundancy and create backups quickly and easily.

3. Optimize PostgreSQL configuration parameters and turn your database server into a high-performance machine capable of fulfilling your needs.

PostgreSQL 9 High Availability Cookbook

ISBN: 978-1-84951-696-9   Paperback: 398 pages

Over 100 recipes to design and implement a highly available server with the advanced features of PostgreSQL

1. Create a PostgreSQL cluster that stays online even when disaster strikes.

2. Avoid costly downtime and data loss that can ruin your business.

3. Perform data replication and monitor your data with hands-on industry-driven recipes and detailed step-by-step explanations.

Please check **www.PacktPub.com** for information on our titles

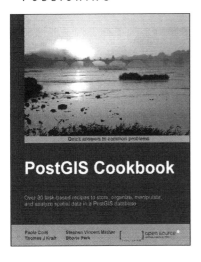
PostGIS Cookbook

ISBN: 978-1-84951-866-6   Paperback: 484 pages

Over 80 task-based recipes to store, organize, manipulate, and analyze spatial data in a PostGIS database

1. Integrate PostGIS with web frameworks and implement OGC standards such as WMS and WFS using MapServer and GeoServer.

2. Convert 2D and 3D vector data, raster data, and routing data into usable forms.

3. Visualize data from the PostGIS database using a desktop GIS program such as QGIS and OpenJUMP.

PostgreSQL Replication

ISBN: 978-1-84951-672-3   Paperback: 250 pages

Understand basic replication concepts and efficiently replicate PostgreSQL using high-end techniques to protect your data and run your server without interruptions

1. Explains the new replication features introduced in PostgreSQL 9.

2. Contains easy to understand explanations and lots of screenshots that simplify an advanced topic like replication.

3. Teaches PostgreSQL administrators how to maintain consistency between redundant resources and to improve reliability, fault-tolerance, and accessibility.

Made in the USA
Middletown, DE
26 February 2017